Profit Theory and Capitalism

PROFIT

POST KEYNESIAN ECONOMICS

A series edited by
Sidney Weintraub

THEORY and CAPITALISM

Mark Obrinsky

University of Pennsylvania Press

Philadelphia 1983

Library of Congress Cataloging in Publication Data

Obrinsky, Mark, 1950–
    Profit theory and capitalism.

    (Post Keynesian economics)
    Bibliography: p.
    1. Profit––History.   2. Economics––History.
3. Capitalism––History.   I. Title. II. Series.
HB601.023 1983   388.5'16'01   82–40482
ISBN 0–8122–7863–1

Printed in the United States of America

to E. L. A. and W. O.

Contents

		Page
PREFACE		xi
1. THE PROFIT PUZZLE		1
2. ADAM SMITH AND THE CLASSICAL CONFUSIONS		10
	Precursors of Smith	10
	Smith's Profit Watershed	12
	Say and the Market	15
	Malthus: Unproductiveness and Profits	17
	Senior's Abstinence	18
	Thünen and the Entrepreneur	20
	Mill: The Attempt at Synthesis	21
3. THE SURPLUS THEORIES: RICARDO AND MARX		27
	Ricardo: The Surplus Product	28
	Marx: Surplus Value as Exploitation	32
4. THE NEOCLASSICAL PROFIT EVASION		39
	Walras's Farewell to Profits	40
	Clark and the Static State	44
	Wicksell: Returns and Profit	47

5. PROFITS AND THE ENTREPRENEUR — 52

Marshall's Managerial Profits — 53
Roscher and Pierson: The Profit Wage — 56
Schumpeter: Innovation and Profits — 60
Hawley and the Risk Theory — 63
Neoclassical Theory: Profit Factors and Equilibrium — 66

6. PROFITS AND UNCERTAINTY — 71

Uncertainty Versus Risk — 72
The Hawley Criticism — 73
The Impact of Uncertainty — 75
Contractual Income — 77
Profit Origin — 79
Entrepreneurs — 81
Profits and Accumulation — 84
Other Uncertainty Theorists — 85
    Burton S. Keirstead — 86
    J. Fred Weston — 87

7. THE INCOMPLETE INSTITUTIONAL VIEW — 93

Contracts and Property — 94
Profits, Entrepreneurs, and Corporations — 97

8. SRAFFA AND THE SURPLUS REVIVAL — 103

Sraffa: Returns and Competition — 104
The Monopolistic Digression — 106
Sraffa: The Surplus Resurrected — 109

9. PROFITS AND THE EARLY MACRO THEORY — 115

Keynes: The Widow's Cruse — 116
Keynes: The General Theory — 120
Boulding's Profit Reconstruction — 122
Kaldor: Keynesian Profits — 127

10. POST KEYNESIAN PROFIT THEORY   133

    Kalecki: Monopoly and Surplus   134
    Robinson: Profits and Capitalism   138
    Weintraub: Uncertainty and Aggregate Supply   143

11. PROFITS: A CONCLUDING ASSESSMENT   153

    Bronfenbrenner's "Naive" Theory   155
    Lamberton and the Firm   156
    Profits and Monitors   157
    Wood's Financial Profits   159
    Profits and General Equilibrium   160
    Profit Theory and Capitalism   162

REFERENCES   169

INDEX   175

Preface

Some four decades ago, when Joan Robinson decided to take a look at the orthodox neoclassical theory of profit, she couldn't find any. When I first began to study the subject less than a decade ago, I found, much to my surprise, that the situation had changed but little. Surely, I had thought, Robinson's discovery would have caused a flurry of activity in profit theory, as many a high-powered theorist sought to be the one to set the matter straight, but this was not the case. This important omission in economic theory seemed to have either gone unnoticed or simply been ignored, with but few exceptions.[1]

Searching for an answer to this perplexing situation, I soon found out that at least part of the answer lay in the difficulty of the problem. But I also discovered that the profit problem had been studied before, at least since Adam Smith, and that some rather interesting and important insights were to be found in the history of economic thought—insights that had apparently not found their way into modern theory. Thus I decided to begin the research which has so far culminated in this volume. My aim was to trace analytically the history of the theory of the origin of profit, with an eye to determining what, if anything, would be useful for a modern profit construction.

It is now my view that mainstream neoclassical economic theory has no real profit theory because it cannot; that is, the presentation

---

1. Most notably Frank Knight and Sidney Weintraub. See Chapters 6 and 10.

of capitalism as an economy in general equilibrium wherein incomes are paid to owners of "productive factors" according to marginal products is antithetical to a meaningful notion of profit. Rather than casting aside the profit concept, as I believe has for the most part happened, that part of economics responsible for reaching this theoretical cul-de-sac must be cast aside, or at least reformulated; those restricting elements that have banished profit must be eliminated. It is also the argument of this book that a suitable framework of analyzing profit can be found in Post Keynesian theory.

While a number of friends and colleagues helped me improve portions of this book, two tower above all others. Karl Niebyl, who has been a constant source of stimulation and a major influence on my intellectual development (more so than he will discern here), is responsible for my first taking an interest in economics. Sidney Weintraub, who through his early confidence in me and by his own energetic example was an indispensable source of inspiration in my coping with the rigors of graduate study, is responsible for first convincing me to look into the subject matter of this book. I gratefully acknowledge my debt to both.

Peoria, Illinois
April 1983

CHAPTER 1

The Profit Puzzle

"When I use a word," Humpty Dumpty said, in rather a scornful tone, "it means just what I choose it to mean—neither more nor less."

"The question is," said Alice, "whether you can make words mean so many different things."

"The question is," said Humpty Dumpty, "which is to be master—that's all."

—Lewis Carroll

It has been recognized at least since Adam Smith that profits are the driving force in a capitalist economy. There are no state planners to issue directives concerning the productive use of the state's resources. Habit, though not without importance, cannot be held responsible for the production and exchange of goods. And benevolence, however widespread, does not supply sufficient inducement for individuals to use their own labor and property in generating output, especially when there is no guarantee of reciprocal benevolence. It is instead the desire for personal gain, the promise of profit, that motivates the entrepreneur to initiate productive activity. "The consideration of his own private profit is the sole motive which determines the owner of any capital to employ it either in agriculture, in manufactures, or in some particular branch of the wholesale or retail trade."[1]

The nature of such profit must therefore be an issue of fundamental importance. It is perhaps surprising, then, to discover that its essence is still very much in dispute. Even more surprising, and certainly disconcerting, is the scant attention paid to this issue, even by theorists whose work necessarily involves (if only implicitly) conclusions and inferences from profit analysis. No doubt this is the result of one peculiarity of profits: as difficult as it is to pin profits down in theory, it is still appealing to think they are easily recognized in the real-world economy, so that the theoretical confusions can be written off as of no practical importance. Such a view seriously underestimates the importance of theoretical clarity, however, as indicated in the examples below.

> Most theoretical economists are used to living amid a welter of diversified and contradictory profit theories. . . . Most of us, I suspect, find the subject so confused as we look about us in the 'real world,' that we have tended to adopt more or less eclectic explanations with varying emphasis on the particular aspect of profit which most clearly satisfies our subjective predilections.[2]

An eclectic explanation, however, is really no explanation, for eclecticism flourishes by mixing opposing, and even contradictory, elements; a consistent, unified theory is thereby precluded. That is also its attraction: difficult problems are allowed to go on unresolved.

The dimensions of this eclecticism and the confusion it creates is illustrated by the usual textbook smorgasbord offered to students of economics. Profit is to be regarded as any or all of the following: implicit rent, interest, and wages; reward for innovation; payment for risk-bearing; the residual in a world of uncertainty; the earnings of monopoly; and exploitation of labor in the Marxist framework.[3] Most of these viewpoints are not compatible with one another; furthermore, important questions are left unanswered (and even unasked). If profits are only implicit factor payments or monopoly earnings, then "pure" profits must be zero. That is, the entrepreneur would receive no payment for his special activity of organizing production. In that case, motivation to continue this activity would vanish and production would cease. A similar result holds for the notion of profits as the payment for risk-bearing. In a world where almost all known risk can be, and usually is, covered by an insurance company, it would appear that only the insurance company would be receiving this profit payment.[4]

Profit as the product of uncertainty presupposes a different conceptual framework. The suggestion that the future is never known, even probabilistically, in advance, and therefore that resource owners have no basis for knowing the future value of their resources, carries with it an inevitable profit precipitate.[5] It also, however, wreaks havoc on equilibrium theory, the consequences of which are all too frequently ignored. The innovational theory reaches a similar abandonment of equilibrium, so long as innovation is continual. If not, neither is profit, which must then be regarded as of "accidental" character, a mere windfall that only temporarily justifies entrepreneurial activity.[6]

Profit as surplus value is another sort of profit explanation altogether. Attention here, as with classical political economy generally, is focused on production rather than exchange, and on the specific form under which it takes place under capitalism. A clear institutional foundation is thus imparted to profit origin. But distinguishing between surplus value, or property income in general, and profit requires a more sophisticated framework than is usually employed in this context.[7]

Clearly there are contradictions here. The factor payment notion, whether implicit or explicit, posits a direct correlation between income and contributions to production. The surplus value theory denies such a correlation, while the uncertainty view finds it impossible to measure (except after the fact, after payments have already been agreed on). Innovation suggests that profits are only temporary, while monopoly implies that they are not general. Thus the student is inevitably left with the impression that profit theory is a morass of confusion better left alone.

With this odd collection serving as profit theory, it is no wonder that "advanced" theoretical models which have entirely abolished profits have a certain appeal. These purport to analyze the economy in general equilibrium where income is paid according to productive contributions, with nothing left for profit (or loss). Why entrepreneurs, who are always frustrated in their attempts to gain profit, should continue to undertake productive activity is left unexplained. Equally unexplained is the distinction between capitalist market economies and other economic systems, distinctions which include prominently (but are not limited to) the profit income. Such models, therefore, represent the triumph of superficial elegance over understanding.

The importance of resolving these problems is easily illustrated. It is a textbook truism that the rate of profit across industries exhibits a tendency toward uniformity (in the absence of monopoly restrictions). This tendency results from the desire to maximize profits and is an important element in the usual explanation of resource allocation. Now the rate of profits is a ratio whose numerator is the amount of profits. It is surely an exercise in futility to try to give meaning to a ratio whose numerator remains unexplained. The denominator is even more problematic. Unless it is determined what the profits are a return to (or for), it cannot be known what the denominator should consist of and the rate of profits simply has no meaning.

Some of the textbook suggestions also present difficulties. If profit is a return for entrepreneurial activity, then the rate of profit must mean the ratio of profits to enterprise. In the case of profit as a reward for innovation, the rate of profit should be taken as the ratio of profit to innovation. In either case, the denominator appears to be unquantifiable. A similar result holds in case profits are a return to monopoly.

The profit rate is in fact usually taken as the ratio of profits to invested capital. The implication is that profits result from, and are a return to, capital. Distinction must, in this case, be made between profit and interest. Problematic is the incorporation of residual income, for if profit is regulated by the amount of capital employed (as it must if it is a return to capital), no income category is left even for the possibility of residuals. Furthermore, this formulation introduces all the difficulties surrounding the concept of capital and its measurement. Both the historical cost of capital equipment and the market value of stocks are of interest to the economist (and even more so to the businessman), but neither is as suitable for profit theory as the current value of capital.[8] The heterogeneity of capital dictates the use of money as the accounting unit. The money value of a capital asset is, however, inseparably linked to its future earnings, discounted by a suitable rate. Now future earnings are necessarily unknown, except in the unrealistic case of perfect foresight or perfect certainty. In addition, the suitable discount rate would be the general rate of return on capital, the rate of profits itself. Unfortunately, it is precisely this rate which is to be determined.[9]

A second simple example will suffice to underscore the theoretical and practical importance of clarity in profit theory. Frequent reference is made to the concept of "normal" profits. It is used in microeconomic theory in conjunction with opportunity costs and is usually built into firms' total cost functions. For policy issues, especially utility regulation, the identification of "normal" profits in large part determines the regulated price. Here again, the issue must be faced: what is the standard of normality? The answer requires a knowledge of the source of profit, for if we do not know what produces profit, we have no basis for determining what is normal and what is not.

It can be objected that there can, even in principle, be no such thing as "normal" profits. Profits generally cover the residual income. In an uncertain world its size can never be known in advance; hence the term "normal" cannot be given any real meaning. There would, of course, be an *ex post* average rate, but this is of little help to either the theorist or the regulator. On the other hand, if profits reward innovation, "normal" profits must have reference to either a "normal" rate of innovation or a "normal" reward for innovation. Both would appear to be contradictions in terms. Furthermore, for "normal" profits to be included as a cost in the output pricing decision, it can only be as a "normal" *rate*. This reintroduces the capital measurement problem just outlined.

It may nevertheless be that actual business decisions are affected by a notion of "normal" profits. If so, the need for theoretical understanding of this concept grows that much sharper.

There is a history to this perplexing state of affairs in profit theory, and a study of that history is indispensable for an understanding of the current dilemma. The various attempts to explain profits have arisen at different times and from different overall analytical perspectives; they are designed, at times, to serve different purposes and answer different questions. A necessary first step in unraveling contemporary confusion is the uncovering of the relevant context within which a particular approach made its appearance. That also supplies the first grounds for testing the adequacy of a theory, namely, whether it is in fact adequate for its designed purpose.

The historical approach must, however, be combined with a critical analysis. A descriptive history can succeed only in providing an appreciation for the complexity of the matter at hand, whereas the task of theory is to make sense of this complexity. Regarding profit theory, this involves separating sense from nonsense, and fruitful from fruitless. Much, probably most, profit theorizing will be seen to fall into the latter categories. There are, however, theories, ideas, insights, and hints of merit. It will be argued here that these can be woven together to produce a useful, integrated profit reconstruction which supplies all that shall be required of profit theory.

It must be emphasized that it is predominately the chronological, rather than the logical, mode of presentation that is adopted here. While this necessitates the consideration of different ideas propounded at different times in a sometimes disjointed fashion, it is more than offset by the advantage of viewing economists in relation to their contemporaries, emphasizing the contributions and limitations of each. It also permits a historical narrative of sorts.

This procedure invites a few brief remarks on the theories considered and the nature of that consideration. In the first place, distinction must be made between genuine analysis and what may be called the "naive" view which appears at various times. In this latter category must be included those writings which simply transfer the regular appearance of profits in the real-world capitalist economy into an unquestioning acceptance of profit as a phenomenon requiring no further explanation.[10] Such a perspective tends to attribute a natural, automatic, even eternal character to profits without inquiring into its causes. It is often found in conjunction with an equally naive cost of production theory of value: the value of a product is equal to the sum of its real costs plus average profits. Unless profits have already been explained, this approach has nothing to offer.

Distinction must also be made between profits as understood by the accountant and profits as understood by the economist. The former clearly include implicit factor returns. While implicit rent, interest, and wages cannot themselves constitute an economist's definition of profit, it remains an open question whether they should be included as part of profit. Many of the classical economists—and some of both their followers and their detractors—followed this approach. In part this is a response to the practical inseparability of implicit factor returns from "pure" profits (no doubt even more difficult in an era of giant corporations). But the aforementioned problem of capital measurement and its relation to profit and interest suggests that it may be even theoretically impossible to distinguish the one from the other. In addition, in a world of uncertainty, the operative concept regarding income distribution is expected, rather than actual, factor returns; implicit returns vanish as a functional notion.

This raises an important methodological problem. It would seem that "as a matter of form, we should start with a definition of what we are talking about. But this, I fear, is the very nub of the whole problem."[11] The defining characteristics of profit to a large extent presuppose the economic framework within which profit is to be analyzed; that is, the adopted definition of profit predetermines the analysis which is to follow. It is common, though by no means universal, to define profit as the income to a firm resulting from the difference between revenue and cost.[12] The difficulty comes both in deciding what should be counted as cost and, more important, in determining why this (positive) differential should occur. Nevertheless, such a view contains what will be considered the essential characteristic of the profit income here: profit is the lone residual income.

This profit-as-residual definition is not meant to be prejudicial to theories involving other views, but rather to clarify the project undertaken. Certainly there must be some income which includes whatever residual appears, even if that appearance is only occasional. For this reason theories that view profit as a return to capital are included, while those that treat the return to capital as interest are not; although the rationale for the existence of an income stemming from capital may be the same, the latter leave open the question of another, residual income, while the former must include the residual as profit, at least implicitly.

This also serves as part of the justification for the treatment of profit theory separately from distribution theory in general. Though it is not denied that the relations between profit and other incomes are close, profit, as the only residual income, has a special character that has no counterpart.

The focus here is on the problem of the *origin* of profit. This is not the only important issue in profit theory, but it is the fundamental one, for if the source of profit is not known, precious little can be said about it. For this reason as well, the analysis will generally be concerned with the economy as a whole rather than with individual firms; or, rather, the analysis of the latter will be in the context of the former. Appropriate supply and demand curves will explain profit to an individual firm, but it is the *ceteris paribus* assumption of those curves that is in need of explanation.

Notes

1. Adam Smith, *Wealth of Nations* (New York: Modern Library, 1965), p. 355.

2. Peter Bernstein, "Profit Theory—Where Do We Go from Here?" *Quarterly Journal of Economics*, August 1953, p. 407. See also Harold Stevenson and J. Russell Nelson, eds., *Profits in the Modern Economy* (Minneapolis: University of Minnesota Press, 1967), p. ix, and Adrian Wood, *A Theory of Profits* (Cambridge: Cambridge University Press, 1975), p. 1.

3. This particular set is taken from Paul Samuelson, *Economics*, 9th ed. (New York: McGraw-Hill Book Co., 1973), pp. 619–24. Substantially the same concoction can be found in most other introductory texts.

4. See Chapters 4 and 5.

5. See Chapters 6 and 10.

6. See Chapter 5.

7. See Chapters 2 and 3.

8. This need not be the same as replacement cost; where they differ, the replacement-cost notion is preferable only for calculations involving the social rate of return.

9. This is one aspect of the well-known Cambridge capital controversy. For a good introduction to the issues involved, see Geoffrey C. Harcourt, *Some Cambridge Controversies in the Theory of Capital* (Cambridge: Cambridge University Press, 1972).

10. The view that profits arise entirely from the exchange process—that is, from buying cheap and selling dear—must likewise be included as a naive view, since it can make sense only in the absence of integrated markets (and hence is not a general phenomenon) or by postulating the existence of a group that buys dear and sells cheap.

11. Bernstein, "Profit Theory," p. 408.

12. Weston, on the other hand, views profit as only a subset of this. See Chapter 6.

CHAPTER 2

Adam Smith and the Classical Confusions

Ce n'est que le premier pas qui coûte.

—*French proverb*

PRECURSORS OF SMITH

Profit theorizing can hardly be said to have begun before Adam Smith's *Wealth of Nations*. Indeed, profit was only beginning to be recognized as a distinct income category. Scant attention had been paid to income distribution in general, and this was concerned with rent and interest. That is only natural, for the profit income is connected with modern capitalist business firms, which were still in their infancy even in the eighteenth century. And the earliest capitalist businesses were associated with commerce, rather than industry; the crucial role of credit in the former made the rate of interest more visible and its analysis more pressing than any possible concern with profit income.

Thus, even the more well-known and perceptive precursors of Adam Smith have little to say on the subject of profit. William Petty analyzes rent and interest, with the latter regarded as a derivative of the former and regulated by it.[1] No mention is made of profit. Dudley North follows Petty in viewing interest as a kind of rent, even referring to it as "Rent for Stock." But while a landlord cannot lose his land in leasing it, a "Stock-lord" does risk his stock, "therefore Land ought to yield less profit than Stock."[2] "Profit" is clearly used generically and does not refer to a special income. The same can be said of John Locke. Comparing rent and interest, he finds that "Money is a barren thing, and produces nothing, but by Compact transfers that Profit that was the Reward of one Man's Labour into another Man's Pocket."[3] It must be remembered, however, that for Locke, labor is the foundation of all property; hence for him, too, profit is not yet a special income category.

Richard Cantillon's position is somewhat more advanced. Profits are the income of "undertakers," a class which includes farmers. An undertaker engages in his business "without assurance of the profit he will derive from his enterprise."[4] Therefore "all Undertakers are as it were on unfixed wages" and "may be regarded as living at uncertainty."[5] This uncertainty derives from the uncertain nature of the market prices at which they will have to sell. Because very little analysis of these prices is undertaken, it remains a mystery why there should ever be profits at all; it appears as a purely fortuitous income. Notwithstanding this fact, Cantillon judges interest to be dependent on profits rather than vice versa.[6] David Hume, by contrast, sees interest and profit to be mutually dependent, though with equally little attempt, as yet, to get at the nature of the profit income.[7]

Anne Robert Jacques Turgot disputes this connection. Although "the industrious man willingly shares the profits of his enterprise with the Capitalist who supplies him with the funds he needs," the rate of interest "is by no means based, as might be imagined, on the profit the Borrower expects to make with the capital of which he buys the use."[8] He adds the reflection that the person who advances capital, whether in agricultural, industrial, or commercial enterprises, "must" receive a profit equal to the wear and tear on their property, "the wages and the price of their labour, their risks, and their industry" and also "the revenue they could acquire with their capital without any labour."[9] While offering a rationale for the capitalist's receiving profit, there is still no explanation for the origin of profit.

Finally, James Steuart discusses profit as an apparent addition to the price of commodities. "In the *price* of goods, I consider two things as really existing . . . the *real value* of the commodity, and the *profit upon alienation.*" The former is determined by the quantity of labor performed, the value of the laborer's subsistence, and the value of the materials. The price of the good can be no lower than this; "whatever is higher, is the manufacturer's profit."[10] This profit is viewed, however, as someone else's loss. "Relative profit is what implies a loss to some body; it marks a vibration of the balance of wealth between parties, but implies no addition to the general stock."[11] As with Cantillon, profit is considered somewhat accidental in character, besides being a species of transfer payment.

Very little, then, has been determined about profit. It is beginning to be seen as an income distinct from rent and interest, though ambiguously so, and somehow related to interest. Nothing has been said about its origin. Such an analysis would require a more comprehensive view of the economy in its totality, as a "circular flow," a self-contained entity separable from the other spheres of human activity. It is this lack that stood in the way of profit theory.[12]

SMITH'S PROFIT WATERSHED

With Adam Smith, profit theory becomes more explicit. Profit is clearly established as a separate and distinct income, and forms, along with wages and rent, one of the three major incomes, interest being relegated to a secondary position. Coinciding with these three incomes are the three classes of society, defined by the income they receive—landlords, laborers, and businessmen (also identified as employers, and as owners of stock). The aim of Smith's investigation, namely, to uncover the causes of a nation's wealth, leads him to examine production, exchange, and the relation between them. This provides a framework in which the inquiry into the origin of profit can, for the first time, have meaning. Finally, Smith is the first to argue clearly the case for an economy motivated not by the conscious satisfaction of needs but by the profit motive.

All this notwithstanding, expectations of finding in Smith a clear and consistent explanation of profit are quickly dashed as his vision is largely directed elsewhere. Threads of profit theory appear, and from them economists as dissimilar as Jean-Baptiste Say and Karl Marx weave profit theories. That they can do so is an indication of the differing perspectives from which Smith opens discussion; their conflict seems to pass unnoticed.

The first to appear is an implicit "surplus" view of profits.[13] This follows from Smith's statement that "the value which the workmen add to the materials, therefore, resolves itself in this case [in which land is excluded] into two parts, of which one pays their wages, the other the profits of their employer."[14] Profits here are a part of the value added by labor, that portion that is left over after deducting wages: profits are the *surplus* over wages. The assignment of wages—at the "subsistence" level—determines profits. Smith does not examine why the laborer should give up as profit what he apparently produces himself; he only mentions the passing of "that early and rude state of society" now that equipment is required and land has become private property.[15] In any case, profit is located here squarely in the sphere of production.

By contrast, Smith also manages a cost of production theory, likewise embedded in his analysis of value. Here "profits of stock constitute a component part" of the price of a commodity, along with wages (in Smith's simple case).[16] Profits are not dependent on wages, but are, rather, independent; instead of decreasing when wages increase, they should hold constant. This requires, of course, some *independent* explanation for the appearance of profit; it no longer suffices to determine wages and prices. Such an explanation is not yet forthcoming.

Smith's crossing over from one position to the other occurs almost without his knowledge. On the one hand, the "profits of stock vary with the price of the commodities in which it is employed"—that is, profits are *not* a fixed component part of price. On the other hand, "high or low wages and profits are the cause of high or low price"—that is, profits *are* a settled component part of price, in a determining sense.[17]

Elsewhere Smith remarks that "profits should bear a regular proportion to . . . capital."[18] He neglects to mention why this should be. It certainly contradicts the surplus notion. There profits depend on the difference between "the value which the workmen add to the materials" and their wages, and therefore not at all on the amount of capital. He is quite right in pointing out that the owner of capital would have "no interest to employ a great stock rather than a small one, unless his profits were to bear some proportion to the extent of this stock."[19] Attempts are later made to turn this observation into a profit theory, though without success. It could be part of an explanation of a tendency toward uniformity in the rate of return on capital, but it fails to explain why there should be any return at all. "Interest" in, or expectation of, profits is hardly adequate cause for their appearance—after all, even those producers who suffer losses must have had "an interest in" making profits.[20]

Smith's confusion is never so great as to permit him to mistake profits for a kind of managerial wage (though both John Stuart Mill and Alfred Marshall, among others, argue along these lines). Profits are, in fact, "altogether different, . . . regulated by quite different principles, and bear no proportion to the quantity, the hardship, or the ingenuity of this supposed labor of inspection and direction."[21]

He also mentions monopoly profits.

The monopolists, by keeping the market constantly understocked, by never fully supplying the effectual demand, sell their commodities much above their natural price, and raise their emoluments, whether they consist in wages or profit, greatly above their natural price.[22]

Smith clearly does not regard monopolies as the primary cause of profit.

Nor does Smith confuse profits with interest of capital, as some accuse.[23] Interest is

the compensation which the borrower pays to the lender, for the profit which he has an opportunity of making by the use of money. Part of that profit naturally belongs to the borrower, who runs the risk and takes the trouble of employing it; and part to the lender, who affords him the opportunity of making this profit. The interest of money is always a *derivative revenue.*[24]

This is a clearer statement of Cantillon's point, yet it still leaves the theory open. One might well ask how the division of this profit between entrepreneur and creditor is effected: are they equal partners in the profits? If not, what principle regulates the division? Smith's answer is a vague reference to the supply of, and demand for, that "stock" which "is destined not only for replacing a capital, but such a capital as the owner does not care to be at the trouble of employing himself."[25] While this may not represent an advance in the theory of interest, neither is it indicative of any misunderstanding concerning interest and profits, even if modern terminology is not employed. Indeed, Smith might have a good case in considering the modern theories, which accord interest on capital a primary place and effect the disappearance of profit, as confused.

SAY AND THE MARKET

Jean-Baptiste Say regards himself as a follower of Adam Smith and views his own role as popularizing (especially for his French audience) as well as organizing and extending the ideas contained in the *Wealth of Nations.* That this is a misleading characterization is nowhere so evident as in his distribution theory, and especially his theory of profits.

Say identifies three major income classes—rent, interest, and wages—which are derived from land, capital, and "human industry." By treating interest as a generalized return to the "productive agency" capital, and not merely as the return to the money lent, he makes a sharp break with Smith (for which he offers no explanation). Partly as a result, he is in a quandary over profits. His "solution" is to consider profits a special type of wage.[26] The difficulties inherent in the approach quickly entangle Say in a web of confusion and inconsistency; the result is instructive, if not immediately constructive.

Say turns to the market to explain profit. Concerning entrepreneurs he remarks: "The price of their labor is regulated, like that of all other objects, by the ratio of supply, or quantity of the labor thrown into circulation, to the demand or desire for it." The supply is limited by two factors. First, the entrepreneur "must at least be solvent," if not in fact self-sufficient in capital, "and have the reputation of intelligence, prudence, probity, and regularity," as well as good business connections. Second, "this kind of labor requires a combination of moral qualities" such as "judgment, perseverance, and a knowledge of the world, as well as of business."[27] Clearly, the number of such men is not large—although Say does not specify how large, or whether men must be born entrepreneurs or instead may acquire entrepreneurial abilities—and if the latter, how.

For the other side of the market, Say relies on derived demand.[28]

When the demand for any product whatever, is very lively, the productive agency through whose means alone it is obtainable, is likewise in brisk demand, which necessarily raises its ratio of value: this is true generally of every kind of productive agency.[29]

Final product demand in turn depends on production: "The general demand for products is brisk in proportion to the activity of production."[30] But if demand depends on supply, it is illegitimate to call upon supply *and* demand to explain entrepreneurial profits (or anything else).

Say's inability to disentangle the workings of the market obscures the fact that the problem is not merely technical. Nowhere is entrepreneurial labor distinguished from labor in general; neither, therefore, are profits distinguished from wages. Say's lone attempt is to suggest that enterprise consists in "the application of acquired knowledge to the creation of a product for human consumption," thereby excluding inventors and innovators.[31] *All* labor may be said to exhibit this characteristic, however. Furthermore, the appearance of losses must force Say to conclude that the entrepreneur in this case was "contributing" something harmful;

on what basis can a distinction in the entrepreneur's efforts be made *ex ante*? No answer is provided by Say.

MALTHUS: UNPRODUCTIVENESS AND PROFITS

Thomas Robert Malthus gets around these difficult profit problems primarily by ignoring them. Even in one of his later works, he offers the following as a definition of "profits of stock."

When stock is employed as capital in the production and distribution of wealth, its profits consist of the difference between the value of the capital advanced, and the value of the commodity when sold or used.[32]

Precisely how this happens is what needs answering. *Why* is the value of the product greater than the value of the capital advanced? Malthus's definition of capital is that "portion of the stock of a country which is kept or employed with a view to profit in the production and distribution of wealth."[33] That is still no help: no doubt the capitalist has "a view to profit," but the economy does not so simply replicate the capitalist's vision. Regarding value, Malthus reverts to the cost of production version of Smith.

Commodities which have cost in their production the same quantity of labour, or the same value of capital, are subject to great variations of value, owing to the varying rate and varying quantity of profits which *must be added* to the quantity of accumulated and immediate labour employed upon them, in order to make up their value.[34]

The issue is why profits should be added. Malthus, like his classical contemporaries, offers scant explanation; profits are simply an assumed fact.

Actually, Malthus also contradicts himself on this point.

The value of commodities in money or their prices are determined by the demand for them, compared with the supply of them. And this law appears to be so general, that probably not a single instance of a change of price can be found, which may not be satisfactorily traced to some previous change in the state of demand or supply.[35]

This principle of supply and demand can, furthermore, "determine . . . the prices of commodities independently of any considerations of cost, or of the ordinary wages, profits, and rent expended in their production."[36] Malthus never even attempts to explain the determination of income as a result of supply and demand, however. Indeed, he is as a rule unaware not only of this inconsistency, but of all the fundamental issues involved.

Malthus does offer something of substance on profit theory, however. This occurs in the context of his defense of the unproductive nature of landlords. Were all workers productive workers, he suggests, who spent their entire earnings on wage-goods (consumption goods), no profit could be made on these goods. Only by positing a class of unproductive workers—or an unproductive class, which would nevertheless have an income—which also required consumption goods, could the price of these goods rise above the wages of the workers who produced them. Strictly speaking, this concerns itself less with the origin of profits as such than with what Marx calls the *realization* of profits. Unfortunately, because his analysis suffers from logical deficiencies, its significance was lost on Malthus's contemporaries; not until the twentieth century (through Keynes's revival) is work along similar lines undertaken.[37]

SENIOR'S ABSTINENCE

Nassau Senior makes the first grand attempt to plug the hole in the cost of production line of reasoning; that is, he tries to discover a productive factor to which profit is the return. Given such a factor, a measurement of its contribution would provide an independent determination of profits, which could then logically be included as a cost. Senior's failure in this attempt is instructive, foreshadowing as it does the inability of any such explanation of a "profit factor" to resolve the issue adequately.

Senior's discovery is "abstinence," or the "act" of not consuming.[38] This abstinence is considered necessary for production and is supposed to be rewarded by the profit income. It is by no means obvious, however, where this income comes from, a fact not sufficiently appreciated by Senior.[39]

Senior admits a different problem, however. The sacrifice involved in waiting for one's income until after the production process is completed is "made by the capitalist, and he is repaid for it by his appropriate remuneration, profit." The size of that remuneration depends on the "proportion which the value of that produce . . . bears to the value of his advances, taking into consideration the time for which those advances have been made." That would appear to have very little to do with abstinence: it is not the sacrifice, the abstaining, of the capitalist that Senior is now pointing to, but rather the positive act of investing. This latter is, however, "necessarily a speculation; it is the purchase of so much productive power which may or may not occasion a remunerative return."[40] Abstinence, as Senior concedes, "may or may not" be rewarded. But with this admission, his profit theory vanishes.

Senior nonetheless assigns a quantitative dimension to all this. Concerning profits, he asserts that both

Profits and Wages . . . are each subject to a minimum and a maximum. They are subject to a minimum, because each of them is the result of a sacrifice. It may be difficult to say what is the minimum with respect to profit, but it is clear that every capitalist, as a motive to abstain from the immediate and unproductive enjoyment of his capital, must require some remuneration exceeding the lowest that is conceivable.[41]

The lowest conceivable, however, is a loss. More important, Senior fails to show how that which is "conceivable" or constitutes a "motive to abstain" is in any way connected to the production of profits.

Trying a different tack, Senior suggests the following.

The facts which decide in what proportions the capitalist and labourer share the common fund appear to be two: *first, the general rate of profit in the Country on the advance of the capital and the receipt of the profit.*[42]

The share of profits in the "common fund" is thus regulated by the rate of profits. But because not only the rate of profits but also their origin itself is unexplained, this comes to naught.

THÜNEN AND THE ENTREPRENEUR

A very different approach is adopted by the German economist Johann Heinrich von Thünen. His decidedly nonclassical focus is on the working out of his "isolated state," in which he briefly examines the activity of the entrepreneur, dropping along the way profit hints that escape his contemporaries.

Profit of enterprise (*Gewerbsprofit*) consists of two parts: *Unternehmergewinn* and *Industriebelohnung*. The former, the gains of the entrepreneur, is what is generally left of revenue after all costs, including interest, insurance premiums, and managerial salaries, have been subtracted. It is by nature uninsurable.

Through the mere fall in the prices of products, manufactures, and commercial commodities, the owner of a good, whether manufacturer or merchant, can lose his entire fortune—and there is no insurance against this danger.[43]

Profit is therefore qualitatively different from all other incomes.

This is diluted somewhat, however, when Thünen suggests that a corporate structure negates this income. Here individuals invest in a variety of corporations, and the fall of some prices will be canceled by the rise of others. For Thünen, this only explains why there are no profits, at least no *Unternehmergewinn*, for corporations. Furthermore, Thünen falls back on the argument that there must be positive profits—at least positive profits must be *expected*, or be *probable*—otherwise the entrepreneur will be reluctant to go into business. True enough, but once again the conditions under which these expectations would be realized are not examined.

The entrepreneur is distinguished from other participants in the productive process also with regard to *Industriebelohnung*. When trouble strikes and one's fortune and honor are at stake, the entrepreneur, unlike salaried help—the "administrator, bookkeeper or overseer"—is preoccupied with one thought only, namely,

how he can avert this misfortune—and sleep flees from him in his bed. . . .
But the sleepless nights of the entrepreneur are not unproductive. . . .
Necessity is the mother of invention, and so too the entrepreneur through
his distress becomes an inventor and discoverer in his sphere.[44]

And the entrepreneur deserves the "rewards" of his inventive
activity just as much as the inventor of new, more productive
machinery (hence the name for this income—"reward of
industry").

There must be some merit in tying profits to an industrial
function of the entrepreneur; Thünen unfortunately does not
suggest how saving one's fortune from *loss* results in positive *gain*.
What is there to guarantee that the entrepreneur will do more than
earn nothing (unless this too would cause "sleepless nights")?
Neither does he indicate whether this income is temporary, because
of competition, or persistent, despite (or because of) the lack of
competition or incessant innovation. This produces, in the end,
merely one more reason for the entrepreneur's "deserving" a profit
reward; the source of this reward is still obscure.

MILL: THE ATTEMPT AT SYNTHESIS

The dual approach to profits in Adam Smith—as a surplus
produced over wages and as an independent component of value—
is elevated by John Stuart Mill into an entire system. More to the
point, Mill attempts to fuse the lines represented by David Ricardo
and Nassau Senior into a single theoretic mold.[45] The synthesis is
incomplete, for Mill actually produces an analytic montage that
proves incapable of firmly supporting any profit theory.[46]

Mill begins with a version of the surplus view. "The cause of
profits is that labor produces more than is required for its support."
This is the surplus theory. Further, "agricultural capital yields a
profit . . . because human beings can grow more food than is
necessary to feed them while it is being grown." Injecting the
notion of the wage fund, Mill adds that if a capitalist "advances"
necessaries to workers "on condition of receiving all they produce,
they will, in addition to reproducing their own necessaries and
instruments, have a portion of their time remaining to work for the

capitalist." Therefore, "profit arises . . . from the productive power of labor."[47]

Mill seems on the verge of enunciating an exploitation theory of profits, but he does not view the process in this light. Wages are simply limited by the number of workers and the *wage fund* (as in the work of his father, James Mill)—that is, that part of capital which consists of subsistence goods ("necessaries") and which equals, therefore, total wages. Mill accepts this as an inevitable law, the only possibility of increasing wages being the reduction in the number of workers who share this fund. Other goods are produced as well, but these somehow represent a different income share. In any case, profits and wages would appear to be in inverse proportion.[48]

In elaborating the value and price of commodities, however, Mill reverts to the opposite approach. Beginning with supply and demand, he ends with the notion that the "necessary price" of a good equals its cost of production *plus* the ordinary rate of profit. Therefore, "if a farmer with a capital equal to 1,000 quarters of corn, can produce 1,200 quarters, yielding him a profit of twenty percent, whatever else can be produced in the same time by a capital of 1,000 quarters, must be worth 1,200 quarters."[49] This is the cost of production side of Smith. It is not logically possible, however, to hold both the cost of production and the surplus views simultaneously. Furthermore, Mill provides no rationale for adding a rate of profit into the price. The businessman might well wish to sell his goods at a markup over costs (if these can be appropriately defined), but there is no *a priori* reason why this price should be sustained in the market. This is precisely what is in need of explanation.

Mill only compounds the confusion by breaking down profits themselves into constituent parts, namely, remuneration for risk, interest on capital, and wages of supervision. Risk will be examined in detail below. Unfortunately, Mill's concept is not particularly helpful; he says little more than that capitalists in industries involving greater risk require greater profit before venturing their capital. He does not suggest that labor in more risky ventures is more productive, however. The inclusion of interest on capital is more interesting. Mill does not have in mind purely money capital, and hence interest in Mill is not what it had been for Smith and Ricardo, purely a return to money. Here, interest is a return to capital generally, that is, to capital in production, and arises from Senior's abstinence. It is still not clear, however, how profit is supposed to arise from "abstaining" from doing something active: Mill is thus no more helpful than Senior.

Furthermore, the *size* of this income from abstinence is at issue. Mill is vague about determining the size of the profit or interest income from either the amount of capital or abstinence. Instead, he reverts to his previous explanation: the capitalist's income is the difference between total product value and the wage fund. Since the calculation of total product value already presupposes knowledge of the rate of profit (at least in Mill's explanation) this reversion lacks explanatory power.

Late in life, Mill retracts the wage fund doctrine—too late for him to assess the implications of the recantation for profit theory. In fact, without it he has no theory at all: if profit is the residual of output value over the wage fund, it is indeterminate in the absence of the latter. Actual wage cost may be substituted, but that requires some other explanation for wages. In the end, not a single piece of Mill's profit structure is left intact.

Notes

1. This despite his view of the value of land as merely capitalized rent. See William Petty, *A Treatise of Taxes and Contributions*, in *The Economic Writings of Sir William Petty* (Cambridge: Cambridge University Press, 1899), pp. 43–45.

2. Dudley North, *Discourses upon Trade* (London: Thomas Bassett, 1691), p. 4.

3. John Locke, *Some Considerations of the Consequences of the Lowering of Interest and Raising the Value of Money* (London: Awnsham & John Churchill, 1969), p. 55.

4. Richard Cantillon, *Essay on the Nature of Trade in General* (New York: Augustus Kelley, 1964), p. 49; see also p. 51.

5. Ibid., p. 55.

6. Ibid., p. 201. Massie emphasizes this, declaring interest to be a part of profits. See Joseph Massie, *An Essay on the Governing Causes of the Natural Rate of Interest* (London: W. Own, 1750), p. 49.

7. David Hume, *Writings on Economics*, ed. Eugene Rotwein (Edinburgh: Thomas Nelson & Sons, 1955), p. 55.

8. *Turgot on Progress, Sociology, and Economics*, ed. Ronald L. Meek (Cambridge: Cambridge University Press, 1973), pp. 159–160.

9. Ibid., pp. 152, 153–154, 157.

10. James Steuart, *An Inquiry into the Principles of Political Economy* (Chicago: University of Chicago Press, 1966), p. 180.

11. Ibid., pp. 159–161.

12. François Quesnay, it can be said, conceives of the economy as such, but has no explicit profit concept yet. Marx nevertheless regards him as analyzing *capitalist* relations, albeit in feudal form. See Karl Marx, *Theories of Surplus-Value*, vol. 1 (Moscow: Progress Publishers, 1963), pp. 44–50.

13. Dobb calls this a "deduction" theory, in contrast to an "adding-up" theory. See Maurice Dobb, *Theories of Value and Distribution Since Adam Smith* (Cambridge: Cambridge University Press, 1973), p. 45, and elsewhere.

14. Smith, *Wealth of Nations* (New York: Modern Library, 1965), p. 48.

15. Ibid., pp. 47–48.

16. Ibid., p. 49.

17. Ibid., p. 146.

18. Ibid., p. 49.

19. Ibid., p. 48.

20. And as Marx later chides, one might "intend" to make profits without producing at all. See Karl Marx, *Capital*, vol. 1 (New York: International Publishers, 1967), p. 191.

21. Smith, *Wealth of Nations*, p. 48.

22. Ibid., p. 61.

23. See, e.g., Frank Knight, *Risk, Uncertainty, and Profit* (Chicago: University of Chicago Press, 1971), p. 23.

24. Smith, *Wealth of Nations*, p. 52; emphasis added.

25. Ibid., p. 334.

26. Besides being awkward, as indicated below, this places him once again at odds with Smith.

27. Jean-Baptiste Say, *Treatise on Political Economy* (Philadelphia: J. B. Lippincott & Co., 1860), p. 330.

28. For more on the problems associated with this approach, see Chapter 4.

29. Say, *Treatise on Political Economy*, p. 324. It should be noted that Say never attempts to sort out the issues involved in the almost all-encompassing case of joint production.

30. Ibid., p. 139. This is one statement of "Say's Law." On this see Thomas Sowell, *Say's Law: An Historical Introduction* (Princeton: Princeton University Press, 1972).

31. Ibid., p. 330.

32. Thomas Robert Malthus, *Definitions in Political Economy* (London: John Murray, 1827), pp. 240–241.

33. Ibid., p. 237.

34. Thomas Robert Malthus, *Principles of Political Economy* (New York: Augustus M. Kelley, 1951), p. 292; emphasis added.

35. Ibid., p. 62.

36. Ibid., p. 70.

37. For references, as well as an interesting assessment of Malthus on this point, see Joan Robinson and John Eatwell, *An Introduction to Modern Economics* (London: McGraw-Hill Book Co., 1973), esp. pp. 25–27.

38. Marshall calls this "waiting," but saving is the most appropriate term.

39. After all, in order for output to exist it is necessary for the workers to "abstain" from destroying the work they have performed. Their "reward," however, consists not in a special profit income but rather in their not being fined or imprisoned. See also Marx, *Capital*, vol. 1, pp. 191–192, 596n.

40. Nassau Senior, *An Outline of the Science of Political Economy* (New York: Augustus M. Kelley, 1951), pp. 93–94.

41. Ibid., pp. 139–140.

42. Ibid., p. 185.

43. Johann Heinrich von Thünen, *Ausgewählte Texte* (Meisenheim, Federal Republic of Germany: Westkulturverlag Anton Haim, 1951), p. 146, translation by William Walker.

44. Ibid., p. 148; translation by William Walker.

45. Though Mill follows Ricardo in time, and in part in analysis, on the issue of profits he contributes more to "classical confusion" than to the surplus theory, hence his inclusion here. Ricardo's analysis appears in Chapter 3.

46. It is little wonder that economists who follow find it necessary to ignore one side or the other. Note that Marx considers that Mill tries to "reconcile irreconcilables." See Marx, *Capital*, vol. 1, p. 16.

47. John Stuart Mill, *Principles of Political Economy* (Fairfield, N.J.: Augustus M. Kelley, 1976), pp. 416–417.

48. This is Ricardo's theorem; see Chapter 3.

49. Ibid., p. 452.

The Surplus Theories: Ricardo and Marx

The working part of this population of 2,500 persons was daily producing as much real wealth for society, as, less than half a century before, it would have required the working part of a population of 600,000 to create. I asked myself what became of the difference between the wealth consumed by 2,500 persons and that which would have been consumed by 600,000. . . .

—Robert Owen

Though no consistent, coherent, and complete theory of the origin of profit has emerged, a beginning has been made. The comprehension of profit as a separate and distinct income is clear in Smith and characterizes subsequent economic analysis. Beginnings are made along several lines that find further expression in the neoclassical era. In particular, the search for a "profit factor" has begun, with Senior's attempt to attribute profit to abstinence. Likewise, the view of profit as a kind of wage is echoed in later views of profit as the reward for a kind of entrepreneurial labor. By contrast, Thünen's effort to discover the special character of the entrepreneur may be seen as leading to theories of uncertainty. Mention has also been made of the "realization" problem that will play an important part in modern macro theories of profit.

More characteristic of classical political economy, however, is the surplus view. Hinted at by Smith, developed into a system by

Ricardo, and transformed by Marx, this view provides a framework in which the issue of profit origin is addressed directly.

RICARDO: THE SURPLUS PRODUCT

Although David Ricardo begins his economic study with inquiries into the problems of money and prices, he soon turns to the issue of profit and distribution. Dividing society into three basic economic classes—"the proprietor of the land, the owner of the stock or capital necessary for its cultivation, and the labourers by whose industry it is cultivated"—Ricardo points out that "in different stages of society, the proportions of the whole produce which will be allotted to each of these classes, under the names of rent, profit, and wages, will be essentially different." His conclusion: "To determine the laws which regulate this distribution, is the principal problem in Political Economy."[1] In shifting the study of profits to center stage in economic theory, Ricardo comes face-to-face with a host of difficult problems that continue to perplex theorists today. Ricardo's contribution is seminal in outlining a method, and a framework, for tackling such problems; this is true despite the shortcomings evidenced in Ricardo, including the inadequate attention paid the issue of profit origin.

Ricardo's first effort at profit theory is contained in what has come to be called the "corn model."[2] Here Ricardo is able to outline a novel theory while escaping the complexities of value theory, essentially by eliminating the heterogeneity of goods that require commensuration. Corn is treated as both input and output in the crucial agricultural sector; that is, corn is both seed for agricultural production and the total of labor's wage, as well as the sole product.[3] The cost of production is thus measured in corn, as is production itself. Paying rent in kind, that is, in corn, allows profit to be calculated in corn, as is also true of the profit rate. The single-good nature of the analysis allows all such measurements to be free from ambiguity.

The wage rate is here taken as a datum and is closely connected to the level of subsistence; thus, if man should require for subsistence double the food previously needed, the expenses of cultivation would be "very greatly increased." Production is determined by technical conditions in the form of the fertility of land under cultivation and existing agricultural techniques and implements. Output is thus given, in corn, by the extent of production—that is, by the amount of labor employed in agricultural production. The costs of production are wages and other circulating capital as well as fixed capital (which includes both tools and buildings). Ricardo treats the value of this latter as also measurable in corn, a more problematic simplification.[4] In this way, however, costs can be directly subtracted from produce, necessary for a determination of profit.

There are three possibilities here. First, "when the whole produce is only equal in value to the outgoings necessary to cultivation, there can neither be rent nor profit." Second, if fertile land is plentiful relative to the needs of the population and output exceeds cost, this net product will appear as profit. Last, if the most fertile land is already being cultivated and the population's food requirements bring more land into production, both profit and rent will be present.[5] The rate of profit in this last case is determined on the least fertile land, where rent is zero. Here, as in the second case, the net product over and above costs is divided by the capital advanced to yield the rate of profit.

This rate of profit on agricultural capital also determines the rate of profit everywhere else.[6] That this is so derives from the nature of the problem. Agricultural profits are determined entirely by the technical conditions that prevail; hence no change in prices or value could have any effect on this rate. Were the profit rate elsewhere less, capital would be transferred into agriculture, bringing still less fertile land into cultivation and changing the technical conditions under which the agricultural rate is determined; nonetheless, it would still be manufacturing and commercial profits that adjust to agricultural profits.[7]

Profits, then, are purely the result of the ability of society, in cooperation with nature, to produce a *surplus*, a product greater than that required to maintain the population. Thus it may indeed be said that profits are "the leavings of wages."[8] Why laborers should, must, or simply do leave this surplus above subsistence to the owners of capital as profit is not examined by Ricardo; it, too, appears simply as institutional fact. Rather, his attention is taken up by the division of the surplus between rent and profit. Barring improvement in the techniques of production, or the import of food, increasing population requiring greater food for subsistence brings increasingly less fertile land into cultivation. As the rate of profit is set on the marginal land, and this is less fertile now than previously, the capital owner suffers a decline in his portion of the produce as that rate falls. This raises rents on all land previously cultivated (including what was previously no-rent land), a part of the surplus produce being transferred from profit to rent. "Rent then is in all cases a portion of the profits previously obtained on the land. It is never a new creation of revenue, but always part of a revenue already created."[9] Progress, understood as the growth of population and capital, inexorably lowers the rate of profit, and therewith the incentive for the capital owner to undertake production.

Clearly, Ricardo's concern is not that his theory may be interpreted as providing a rationalization for labor to deny the businessman his profit, but rather that the landlord is already doing just that. The reasons for, and the significance of, the falling profit rate receive, therefore, almost all of Ricardo's attention. His recognition that the conclusion depends on the simplification involved in the one-sector model he is using, and his desire to show the generality of the conclusion, lead him to develop the analysis under the real-world condition of heterogeneous commodity inputs and outputs. This requires that the problems of value theory be resolved; hence value theory is where Ricardo opens his *Principles*.

The solution is a labor theory of value. By determining the value of commodities by the amount of labor required to produce them (modified by the durability of capital and the proportion of fixed capital to circulating capital), Ricardo is still able to measure both input and output, now consisting of sets of different goods, in a consistent manner. Furthermore, he is once again able to settle this question of values and costs prior to the determination of profits. Thus, the value of the product is determined by the amount of labor embodied in it, the wages of labor are determined by the amount of labor necessary to produce subsistence, and profit arises from the difference. That there is a profit potential results from the ability of the laborer to produce more than subsistence, which Ricardo apparently understands as a technological fact. This follows from the absence of further discussion on this point, as well as from the problem that crops up here in his value theory. If labor expended determines value, the value of labor itself, or wages, should be the labor expended in the production of labor, an expression without meaning.[10] Ricardo's fixing of wages at subsistence then requires other grounds, though he seems not to notice, never commenting directly on this point. It is clear, however, that the possibility of profit (and rent) must vanish should labor as a class receive the entire product, a situation Ricardo identifies with productivity being such as to permit the population to just meet its subsistence requirements.

The problem is not so easily resolved, however. The productivity of labor by itself would lead to labor either not working beyond the point required to produce subsistence, or else living above the subsistence level; in either case, profits do not exist as a separate income category. To put the matter differently, it is not clear why the price of a good should exceed its labor cost (due account being taken for the labor required to produce capital goods). Ricardo confronts this problem indirectly in analyzing the impact of differing amounts of fixed capital employed in production. His illustration makes this clear.

A cloth manufacturer employs one hundred men in one year to produce a machine and then in the following year to produce, with the aid of the machine, cloth. A farmer employs one hundred men to produce corn one year, and the same the next. Wages are £50 per year, and profits are 10 percent per year. Then the cost of the machine and the corn at the end of the first year is £5,000 apiece (one hundred workmen at £50) and the value is £5,500 (£5,000 plus 10 percent profits). The second year the farmer again has his corn of £5,500, but the manufacturer, "to be on a par with the farmer, must not only obtain £5,500 . . . but must obtain a further sum of £550 for the profit on £5,500" which he has invested in machinery, raising the value of his goods to £6,050.[11] The manufacturer has in effect invested his profit of the first year into his production, whereas the farmer has evidently consumed his.

This example is presented as a modification of the theory that labor alone determines relative values, but in fact it serves another purpose as well. A rise in wages, which effects a fall in the rate of profits, actually lowers the price of the manufactured cloth relative to the corn. For Ricardo, this is a demonstration of the falsity of the component parts theory of value. In the latter, a fall in profits should operate equally across industries, leaving relative prices unchanged.

Ricardo does not, however, offer any clear explanation of where the manufacturer's extra £550 comes from, any more than he explains where the farmer's 10 percent profit comes from. Certainly profits are not seen as connected with the notion of productivity of capital as a factor of production. To be sure, capital may be productive and thus reduce the labor required to produce subsistence, hence also the value of the wage; profits would then rise. But this is in no sense a return to capital as a productive factor. Unfortunately, this leaves unexplained the very vital origin of the profit income.

MARX: SURPLUS VALUE AS EXPLOITATION

Marx, who like Ricardo adopts a labor theory of value, must resolve the obscurities in the latter's theory. First this means clearing up the "value of labor" problem. For Marx, not labor but labor power is the relevant commodity; the worker sells to the owner of capital not his work but his ability to do work. Since the ability to work depends on the continued physical existence of the laborer, which in turn requires food, clothing, shelter, and so on, the value of this labor power is the labor necessary to produce subsistence goods.[12] This eliminates the inconsistency of Ricardo.

Labor power is a unique commodity, however, in that its consumption—the performance of labor by the laborer—not only produces value but also produces more value than it has; that is, the laborer adds more value to production than is required for his subsistence.[13] The extra margin is defined by Marx as surplus value and is clearly a matter of exploitation. Although again the existence of surplus value is dependent on a certain level of productivity, the latter is only a necessary, but not a sufficient condition for the former.[14] Surplus value arises only under the specific social relations of property identified with capitalism. Thus, labor power is a commodity only because it has been divorced from the means of laboring, or means of production, which are in the hands of another class (which, as a consequence, does not perform labor).[15] Furthermore, Marx refers to the process of surplus value production as merely the quantitative extension of the process of the production of value (equal to the value of labor power).[16] Technology may provide the possibility, but capitalist institutions provide the necessity for surplus value to be produced.

Surplus value is not identical to profit, however.[17] The latter is just one of the incomes to which the former gives rise, the others being rent and interest.[18] Profit is the residue after the deduction of rent and interest; that is, the various property incomes arise from the sharing of surplus value among the owners of various kinds of property. There are no laws, or long-run tendencies, which can determine quantitatively the amount of profit, because the rate of interest has no "natural" value. That is, the interest rate is purely "accidental," is not subject to determination by any definite law.[19] To a degree, the same is true of rent. Marx sees not only the differential rent of Ricardo, but also an absolute rent. The latter results from landed property—that is, from the private ownership of land by a distinct class. Absolute rent presupposes, for Marx, a distinction between value and price, however, a phenomenon also connected to the problem Ricardo saw as modifying his theory that labor embodied determines value.

Marx recognizes that if commodities sell at their labor values, and if surplus value depends only on the amount of labor ("variable capital") but not on "constant capital"—that part of the capital advanced going to machines and raw materials—then the different capital/labor ratios across industries will necessarily produce different rates of return on capital invested in different industries. This contradicts the fact of competition of capital which tends to equalize the rate of profit. The solution is that goods are in fact exchanged not at their values but at "prices of production." The latter are based on the former, but involve, in general, deviations from them. In particular, these prices are determined so that the total surplus value is distributed to the different individual capital outlays according to their total size rather than according to variable capital alone, as is the case with the determination of value. That is, the total surplus value is compared with the total capital outlay to get an overall rate of profit. This rate of profit is then added to the value of the capital advanced in each production process to get the price of each good. Total profit will equal total surplus value, and the sum of the values of the goods produced will equal the sum of their prices of production.[20]

This is cited by Eugen von Böhm-Bawerk as the great contradiction in Marx; after all, prices either are equal to labor values, or they are not, in which case the labor theory of value is not really a theory of value at all.[21] For Marx, however, the assertion that goods exchange at their prices of production depends on the prior construction of the labor theory, and hence is legitimately a modification, not a contradiction. The analogy would be the relation of air resistance to Newton's law of free-falling objects: air resistance abolishes neither the law nor the fact of gravity. For Marx, always lurking behind the actually existing general rate of profit is labor value. Marx never completes the "transformation" of values into prices, but only indicates that it can be done.[22]

This view then "adds" profit into the price, but only after determining the amount to add in by the labor theory, and after explaining the origin of this profit in the exploitation of the laborer. The deviation of price from value also accounts for the possibility of absolute rent. The distribution of surplus value effected by the shift from values to prices is from those sectors with lower-than-average capital/labor ratios ("organic composition of capital") to those with higher-than-average capital/labor ratios. Agriculture, as a rule, has a lower-than-average capital/labor ratio; hence, agricultural prices are lower than agricultural values. Since landed property prevents any land from being cultivated without paying rent, even the worst land, the existence of absolute rent implies (1) the existence of rent on the worst land being cultivated, in contradiction to the Ricardian theory, and (2) the existence of some "fund," or revenue, from which it is paid. Marx finds it in the surplus value that would otherwise be divided up among all capital investors. "Landed property hinders . . . an equalisation among capitals invested in land, whenever production requires land for either agriculture or extraction of raw materials, and takes hold of a portion of the surplus-value, which would otherwise take part in equalizing to the general rate of profit."[23]

The extent of absolute rent (along with differential rent and interest) affects the amount of surplus value remaining with the capitalist in the form of profit of enterprise. How great it can be "depends upon the relative development of agriculture as compared with industry."[24] This, however, is not a predictable phenomenon, at least in the relevant time frame; hence for this reason, too, the size of profit is not a strictly determinable magnitude. In no case does Marx view profit as disappearing. This would require that interest and rent grow so large that they entirely consume profits, a situation that would cause the elimination of production—that is, of capital employed productively, and would therefore work against both the creditor and the landlord as well as the borrower-capitalist.

None of this would matter if the commodities produced could not be sold—that is, if the profit that has been produced is not also "realized." While this is clearly important for Marx, it is not directly connected to the problem of profit origin; the latter concerns production alone. By contrast, realization is a matter of exchange, and it leads Marx to his familiar equations of proportionality required for uninterrupted accumulation of capital.[25]

Marx also speaks of the law of the tendency of the rate of profit to fall. Of course, for the rate of profit to reach zero, both profit and surplus value would have to vanish. This is not what Marx has in mind, however. After enunciating this law, he quickly cites counteracting forces, thereby dispelling any notion of an irreversible, monotonic fall. The mechanism of the falling profit rate also suggests the permanence of profit: increasing capital designed to increase the rate of surplus value—surplus value divided by wages—which increases the denominator in the profit rate. Thus, the profit rate falls despite an increase in the absolute amount of profits.[26]

Less well known are his comments, admittedly brief, on uncertainty and its role in the economy. They nevertheless deserve mention in the light of subsequent economic analysis.

For Marx, uncertainty, other than that arising from man's

imperfect knowledge of nature, is a consequence of commodity production—by which Marx understands private production for the market. By his very nature, a private producer cannot know in advance if his own production method will make his costs greater, less, or the same as the industry-wide average. Similarly, he cannot know in advance the conditions, both demand and supply, existing in the market when he is ready to sell his product.[27] These things he can know only after the production process, when he actually tries to sell the product at a profitable price. The result is uncertainty on the part of the producer as to both market price and salable quantity. Or, as Marx puts it,

> Commodities are direct products of isolated independent individual kinds of labour, and through their alienation in the course of individual exchange they must prove that they are general social labour, in other words, on the basis of commodity production, labour becomes social labour only as a result of the universal alienation of individual kinds of labour.[28]

Marx, however, never sees this uncertainty as a source of profits, except temporarily. He argues, as so many before and after, that competition tends to eliminate this sort of profit. This is somewhat at variance with his usually dynamic perspective; indeed, the elimination of these profits of "dynamic error" is tantamount to the elimination of uncertainty. An alternative interpretation would be simply that Marx believes profits to originate primarily from exploitation of labor; the profits and losses due to uncertainty are secondary features of the market economy.

Notes

1. David Ricardo, *Principles of Political Economy and Taxation*, in *The Works and Correspondence of David Ricardo*, ed. Piero Sraffa, vol. 1 (Cambridge: Cambridge University Press, 1951), p. 5.

2. Piero Sraffa clarifies the development of this "corn theory" and dates its first working-out by Ricardo at 1814. See his "Introduction," ibid. For another view, see Samuel Hollander, *The Economics of David Ricardo* (Toronto: University of Toronto Press, 1979), as well as the critical review by Alessandro Roncaglia, "Hollander's Ricardo," *Journal of Post Keynesian Economics*, Spring 1982, pp. 339–59.

3. David Ricardo, "An Essay on the Influence of a Low Price of Corn on the Profits of Stock," *Works*, vol. 4, p. 15. Ricardo refrains from asserting explicitly that the wage is just sufficient to cover subsistence and that the wage is made up entirely of corn. This appears to be his general meaning, though he clearly regards it as a simplification of reality.

4. E.g., "if the capital employed by an individual in such land were of the value of two hundred quarters of wheat, of which half consisted of fixed capital, such as building, implements, etc. . . ." *Works*, vol. 1, p. 10.

5. Ibid., pp. 10–13. A fourth possibility, that of rent but no profits, is examined below.

6. Ibid., p. 12. See also Sraffa's comment, ibid., p. xxxi.

7. The reverse argument holds in case the agricultural profit rate is below that elsewhere.

8. Thomas de Quincey, *The Logic of Political Economy* (Edinburgh and London: William Blackwood & Sons, 1844), p. 204; quoted in Maurice Dobb, *Theories of Value and Distribution Since Adam Smith* (Cambridge: Cambridge University Press, 1973), p. 18

9. *Works*, vol. 4, p. 18.

10. Bailey's criticism of Ricardo on this point is logically correct. See Samuel Bailey, *A Critical Dissertation on the Nature, Measure, and Causes of Value* (London: R. Hunter, 1825), pp. 50–51.

11. *Works*, vol. 1, pp. 34–35.

12. Marx, like Ricardo, views subsistence not as physically determined but rather as historically and culturally determined, albeit with a physical minimum.

See Karl Marx, *Capital*, vol. 1 (New York: International Publishers, 1967), p. 171.

13. Ibid., p. 193.

14. Regarding the former, see Karl Marx, *Theories of Surplus-Value*, vol. 1, (Moscow: Progress Publishers, 1963), pp. 48–49.

15. Ibid., pp. 168–70.

16. Ibid., p. 195.

17. Although Marx frequently uses the term "profit" as if it were the same as the total of property income (which corresponds to surplus value), he does so only by abstracting from other property incomes for simplification in the analysis and exposition; conceptually they remain distinct.

18. Actually, Marx also distinguishes "commercial profit" from "profit of enterprise." The latter is the residual and prior to the former; here "profit" refers to this "profit of enterprise."

19. *Capital*, vol. 3, p. 364.

20. *Capital*, vol. 3, pp. 154ff.

21. See Eugen von Böhm-Bawerk, *Karl Marx and the Close of His System* (New York: Macmillan Co., 1898).

22. This conclusion has held up in the voluminous debate on this transformation problem, though the assertion that *both* the sum of values equals the sum of prices *and* total profits equal total surplus value has been shown to be true only under special circumstances. See Ronald Meek, *Studies in the Labor Theory of Value* (New York: Monthly Review Press, 1956). See also the bibliographies (and articles) of Paul Samuelson in the *Journal of Economic Literature*, June 1971, pp. 429–31; David Laibman in *Science and Society*, Winter 1973–74, p. 494; and M. Morishima and G. Catephores, in the *Economic Journal*, June 1975, pp. 327–28.

23. *Capital*, vol. 3, p. 771.

24. Ibid., p. 772.

25. Contrast Kalecki's view of the relation of realization of profit to its origin. See Chapter 9.

26. See *Capital*, vol. 3, chaps. 13, 14.

27. Marx is clearly not interested in the case of an already existing static equilibrium.

28. Marx, *A Contribution to the Critique of Political Economy* (New York: International Publishers, 1970), pp. 84–85.

CHAPTER 4

The Neoclassical Profit Evasion

There are certain saving clauses in common use . . . : "Given the state of the industrial arts"; "Other things remaining the same"; "In the long run"; "In the absence of disturbing causes." . . .

Now . . . the state of the industrial arts has at no time continued unchanged during the modern era; consequently other things have never remained the same; and in the long run the outcome has always been shaped by disturbing causes. All this reflects no discredit on the economists and publicists who have sketched out the natural run of the present and future in the dry light of 18th-century principles, since their reservations have not been observed. . . . The fault appears to lie in the unexampled shifty behavior of the latterday facts.

—*Thorstein Veblen*

With the 1870s, neoclassical analysis emerges as the mainstream vision. Perhaps its essential characteristic is its turn toward the (perfectly competitive) market as the key to understanding economic phenomena. The turn away from production as the basis of the economy also means dropping the surplus notion, which can be understood only as a phenomenon of production. This transforms both the theory of value and the theory of distribution: it is the market which now explains income. Wages, interest, and rent—the incomes of the three great factors of production labor, capital, and land—are large or small according to whether the productive services they provide are valued high or low. The value of each productive factor, and therefore its income, is "derived" from the value of the consumer goods they directly or indirectly produce.

This derived value, based on "derived demand," ostensibly arising from the Ricardian theory of rent, forms the basis for distribution theory in the postclassical world.[1]

In this new economic world, the opportunity for profit narrows considerably. There are only two possibilities: either there is a fourth productive factor, whose services are rewarded by the profit income, or profit exists only because of imperfections that keep the three factors from receiving the full income they have generated. Neoclassical theory tends in the main to cling to the latter position, though some writers look for profit in the special activity of the entrepreneur.[2]

As a result, profit theory is set to one side, removed from the core of economic theory; little attention is accorded profit theory in the analysis of the economy. William Stanley Jevons, for example, mentions profits only briefly, resolving them into "wages of super-intendence, insurance against risk, and interest."[3] The wage is a return to labor, the risk premium equalizes the result in different employments, and the interest is a return to capital and is every-where equal; only temporarily can there be a positive residual income beyond this.[4] Karl Menger has even less to say, and Böhm-Bawerk states explicitly: "I shall . . . purposely refrain from investigating or deciding the problem of the entrepreneur's profit," to which position he is faithful.[5] And with Leon Walras profit vanishes altogether.

WALRAS'S FAREWELL TO PROFITS

Walras's theory is a comprehensive mathematical system of general equilibrium, indeed, the first such system.[6] No examination of any facet of this theory of the market economy would be comprehensible except in its relation to the entire system. The central role in this system is played by the market. For Walras, "*pure economics* is, in essence, the theory of the determination of prices under a hypothetical regime of free competition."[7] As will become clear, however, the analysis implicitly involves much more than price theory.

Walras distinguishes three different types of markets within the general system: the market for consumer goods, the market for productive services, and the market for new capital goods. In the first, individuals come to the market owning certain amounts of various commodities and having the intention of exchanging them against other commodities according to their own wants and desires and according to prevailing prices. There will be a single set of commodity prices at which equilibrium prices can be established, effective offer equaling effective demand for all commodities.

To arrive at this otherwise imaginary equilibrium, Walras has recourse to an auctioneer, who shouts out potential prices, takes note of inequalities of offer and demand, adjusts prices accordingly, and through this process of groping (*"tâtonnement"*) reaches the equilibrium position. Walras is aware, of course, that this auctioneer is equally imaginary.[8]

In the second market, workers, capitalists (capital owners), and landowners offer the services of the productive factors they own. Entrepreneurs buy these services (or, the equivalent, hire the productive factors) for the purpose of production, whose products they intend to sell in the first market. Presumably, they hope to make a profit. With this, Walras completes the analytic separation of entrepreneur from capital owner (and of profits from interest on "capital").

It is clear that the prices entrepreneurs are willing (or able) to pay for productive services depend on the prices of products; this second market, therefore, would appear to be logically dependent on, "derived" from, the first. Walras seems to say as much: although "productive services are bought and sold in their own special markets, nevertheless the prices of these services are determined in the market for products."[9] In general, however, Walras presents his system as one of general interdependence and simultaneous determination rather than one-way determination; it is not clear how he would want to resolve this apparent contradiction in interpretation.[10] In any case, Walras again shows the existence of an equilibrium position, and again arrives at it through his auctioneer, this time aided by *bons*, "tickets."

In this production equilibrium, entrepreneurs make "neither profit nor loss," for the following reason: if, for example, one entrepreneur were making a profit, other entrepreneurs would turn to this industry, thereby expanding production (or the one entrepreneur would expand production himself), which would lower prices and eliminate profits.[11] This is at first a rather surprising conclusion. The correct conclusion would seem to be that the rate of profits tends to be equalized across industries, producing a uniform rate; indeed, this is how the same example is used before (and after) Walras.[12] It is quite another matter to assert that this uniform rate is actually equal to zero. Walras must use here his distinction between capitalist and entrepreneur. Clearly, if capital ownership were required to enable one to become an entrepreneur (as the classical theorists generally suggest), the number of entrepreneurs would be strictly limited, and the zero-profits situation would be merely a very special case.[13] In Walras's scheme, however, anyone can become an entrepreneur.[14]

Although this market determines the prices paid for the productive services, *inter alia* interest, there is clearly no *rate* of interest as yet, nor can there be until there is a price for capital. Since that price is nothing but the capitalized future earnings of capital and therefore depends on the rate of interest, there is another potential source of difficulty, namely, prevision and foresight. In any case, none of this can be determined unless there is a market for capital goods. Since buying and selling already-existing capital goods is irrational under equilibrium (since there is no gain to be had either way), Walras turns to the market for new capital goods.

Here "new capital goods are exchanged against the excess of income over consumption," or savings, which is a function of prices and the rate of interest, and "the condition of equality between the value of the new capital goods and the value of the excess gives us the equation required for the determination of the rate of net income [interest] and consequently for the determination of the prices of capital goods."[15] Positive savings, as the condition for a growing economy, thereby occur by way of *assumption*. It follows, therefore, that a positive rate of interest also arises by assumption. Walras's system is, as a result, designed not to explain the emergence of a positive rate of interest but merely to determine its size while taking for granted its existence. Whether Walras succeeds in doing even this is a point of contention, though not one at issue here.[16]

Walras is explicit about the existence of profits in this system. As indicated, Walras stipulates that "in a state of equilibrium in production, entrepreneurs make neither profit nor loss. They make their living not as entrepreneurs, but as land-owners, laborers or capitalists in their own or other businesses."[17] Elsewhere he says,

So far as profit is concerned, in the sense of profit of enterprise, the English classical school fails to see that it is the correlative of possible loss, that it is subject to risk, that it depends upon exceptional and not upon normal circumstances, and that theoretically it ought to be left to one side.[18]

Since, however, in reality profit is the "normal" (i.e., commonly occurring) case, one must ask why it should be put aside, where this theory has gone astray, or which of its features has led to this no-profit conclusion as a logical outcome.

Some of the difficulties have already been indicated. Perhaps the main problem involves Walras's central concept—general equilibrium. Walrasian equilibrium is a manifestly unreal phenomenon: not only is it purely ideal in the sense that the real-world economy is never actually in such a state, but it is also purely ideal in the sense that the process by which Walrasian equilibrium is reached is one that cannot be duplicated in the real world. This is because both *time* and *uncertainty* enter inexorably into real-world affairs, yet both have been eliminated by Walras.

The significance of this omission can be grasped from an analysis of the market for productive services. In order for the entrepreneur to know what to bid for the productive services, he must already know the selling prices of products. In the Walrasian system, he learns this by a timeless process of trial and error involving an auctioneer and tickets. Even if the real-world economy could operate as an equilibrating force, it could not do so timelessly, for production is separated from sale of products chronologically as well as institutionally. This being so, the general equilibrium position Walras describes could be reached only through perfect foresight. Uncertainty, however, rules the real world (uncertainty not in an absolute sense, but in the sense of less-than-perfect foresight or incomplete conviction concerning anticipations).

Walras evidently does not recognize this problem.

Equilibrium in production, like equilibrium in exchange, is an ideal and not a real state. It never happens in the real world. . . . Yet equilibrium is the *normal state* in the sense that it is the *state towards which things spontaneously tend* under a regime of free competition in exchange and production.[19]

This statement is more an article of faith than a validated conclusion.

Another significant problem is that although profit is considered to be a return to an enterprise or firm (over and above the return to the productive factors that may be intertwined), nowhere does Walras explicitly discuss the firm or its special role, if any, in the economy. The clear implication is that neither the firm nor the entrepreneur plays any role at all, except as an equilibrating mechanism. One might expect such an assertion to be documented; even in 1874, before the advent of the large corporation, the firm was not an invisible agent.

This point can be carried further. The Walrasian entrepreneur borrows someone else's physical capital (or, rather, buys the services of someone else's physical capital), for which he must pay interest, which, along with rent and wages, exhaust the value of the product. If instead the firm is viewed as a borrower of money capital with which it purchases its own physical capital, then the no-profit situation is one in which the rate of interest on money capital equals the rate of return on physical capital. This might be true in the Walrasian equilibrium, but it is not the only possible equilibrium solution. And it is certainly not true once time and uncertainty are admitted into the analysis.

CLARK AND THE STATIC STATE

In order to explain the origin of profits, John Bates Clark has recourse to an explicit theory of economic dynamics. This he contrasts to the theory of universal economic laws, applicable to all past and future economies, and to a theory of economic statics. The three together comprise economic theory in its entirety. Unfortunately, his full exposition of dynamics—as is still too often the case—remains an unfulfilled promise, while his textual analysis is confined to the brief treatment that appears in his exposition of distribution theory.[20]

The static state is one in which production and exchange take place unchanged: there is replacement of worn-out productive equipment, and new laborers take the place of old; but there is no net capital increase. Alternatively, the five sources of progress or dynamic change are absent: increase of population, increase of capital, improvements in technology, improvements in industrial organization, and changes in wants. Clark recognizes that such a static state is not found in the real world; nevertheless, a study of its laws is necessary, because the same laws operate in the dynamic state as well, even if not by themselves. "All the forces that would work in the unchanging world are not only working in the changeful one, but are even the dominant forces in it."[21] The latter point turns out to be mere assertion, however.

For this static state, Clark works out the laws of marginal productivity for which he is remembered.[22] He considers capital and labor to be the two productive factors that earn incomes in the static state; land is only a species of capital (indeed, rent and interest are identical incomes, considered, however, from different points of view). In this state there is no room for profit. Here the prices of goods are stabilized at their "natural," "normal," "static," or "cost-" prices, and "cost-prices are, of course, no-profit prices. They afford, in the case of each item, enough to pay wages for the labor and interest on the capital that are used in working it; but they give no net surplus to the entrepreneur as such.[23] Unfortunately, Clark nowhere gives an explicit account of why there are no profits in the static state, which, therefore, remains an assumption.[24]

In this state, competition acts as the great leveler which assures that units of labor and capital everywhere produce the same amount. Wages then are governed by the marginal product of labor, interest by the marginal product of capital. (Clark actually seeks to show not merely that the product of the "last" worker—a mental imprecision on Clark's part—is the rule which governs payment of all workers, but that each worker in fact receives "all" that he produces.[25]) Unlike Walras, Clark is concerned to represent this as a real process, and he consequently allows time into the consideration of the economy. Time is here no more than the repetitive flow of identical events, however; it becomes meaningful only in the context of the dynamic state.

At the same time, it must be noted that by presenting the development of the static state as a process in which events are time-ordered (even if it is an imaginary time), Clark explicitly introduces causality. The chain of determination traps him in some difficulties. The most important of these is the circularity involved in presenting marginal productivity as a macro theory of distribution; if the value of capital is equal to the discounted sum of its future earnings, it depends on the rate of interest, and therefore Clark's procedure of having competition equalize the products of, and therefore the return to, units of capital becomes invalid as a means of determining the rate of interest.

Clark then considers the dynamic state in light of the analysis of the static state. The five dynamic changes he enunciates have two main effects: (1) The standards for wages and interest—arrived at in the static state—change; that is, the parameters for the static distribution solution are different. (2) The *actual* wages and interest being paid at any moment differ from their static standards; the economy, that is, cannot instantaneously shift from one set of "static" standards to another. While Clark considers the former effect to be more important, it is the latter which produces profits. An example appears in his views on new technology. "An invention makes it possible to produce something more cheaply. It first gives a profit to entrepreneurs." However, the static laws begin to take over, and turn the profits into wages and interest—"from the moment when the improved method has been put into operation the static standard of wages has been higher." Dynamic change, therefore, produces profit, but only temporary profit, which the laws of the static state rapidly eliminate. Thus, profit "is an *elusive* sum, which entrepreneurs *grasp, but cannot hold.*"[26]

There are two kinds of difficulties associated with this view of profits. The first concerns the ability of Clark's dynamic changes to actually produce profits. Frank Knight argues that it is not change as such which is capable of producing profit, but rather its unforeseen character. With "general foreknowledge of progressive changes no losses and no chance to make profits will arise out of them. This is the first principle of speculation. . . . The effect of any change which can be foreseen will be adequately discounted in advance."[27] It is uncertainty, therefore, which is responsible for profit.

The other obstacle is Clark's conception of the dynamic state. This state is nothing more than a series of static states, whose laws Clark considers dominant. Though he makes many suggestive references to physical phenomena, he never provides any supporting argument to explain why this should be so in the real-world economy. Thus, in examining the mobility of labor in the static state, Clark indicates that it may well take a generation for competition to equalize the products of various laborers. Certainly an increase of population takes no longer. Similarly, if a particular capital good lasts twenty-five years, it may well take that long for the mobility of capital to work itself out fully. Clearly, technological change occurs faster than that (even in his day).

Nor does Clark ever question the influence of dynamics on the laws of the static state. Surely real-world competition does not operate as Clark supposes it does in his static model; in particular, it can actually lead to monopoly, through collusion (as even Adam Smith recognizes) or through the defeat (i.e., bankruptcy) of some in the competitive struggle.

It is therefore not at all obvious that the dynamic state can be accurately understood through the telescope of the static one. And in the end, Clark's profits (like Walras's) exist only to be eliminated by inexorable economic forces. For Clark the capitalist economy is driven to abolish profits, whose origin therefore resides in the inability of capitalism to perform its task perfectly.

WICKSELL: RETURNS AND PROFITS

If in Clark the entrepreneur earns profit, temporarily, due to dynamic forces, in Knut Wicksell the entrepreneur ceases to perform any function at all; small wonder, then, that he also receives no income for doing this.

Wicksell treats three factors of production—land, labor, and capital, once again—and the three economic classes associated with them: landlords, laborers, and capitalists. They must be brought together for production to take place. This organizing of production, however, presents no formidable problem; it requires no particular talents. And therefore it can be done by anyone. That is why, in his *Lectures on Political Economy*, Wicksell considers both "The Landowner as Entrepreneur" and "The Labourer as Entrepreneur" (capital being temporarily ignored) and finds no essential distinguishing features.[28] Elsewhere, he is even more explicit, even when capital is included. He describes landlords hiring capitalists and workers, and capitalists hiring workers and landlords, and then imagines workers hiring landlords and capitalists. Precisely the same equilibrium position would be reached.[29]

It is not surprising, then, to find that Wicksell considers it

obvious that entrepreneurial profits as such must always tend to zero. For the work and thought which the entrepreneur devotes to the management of production, he should, of course, receive wages like any other worker. If he also uses property . . . he will of course receive a corresponding share of the product . . .

as would any property-owner. But that is as far as it goes, for "if he were to obtain a share of the product in his capacity of entrepreneur, it seems likely that the whole world would rush to obtain *income so easily acquired.*" What follows, however, is a proof of the necessity of constant returns to scale for this result to be valid; and "this assumption [constant returns] is far from obvious or generally valid; on the contrary, it may be questioned whether it is ever strictly fulfilled. . . ."[30]

This is repeated later. In considering "non-capitalistic production"—that is, production with land and labor only—he asks if "nothing is left over for the entrepreneur as such." His reply is that although this proposition may seem evident in "abstract theory," it depends, in practice, on constant returns to scale (or that an enterprise is in an intermediate position between increasing and decreasing returns).[31] When treating "capitalistic production," however, he concerns himself with the return to *capital*—that is, interest—and not with profit. Here, he follows Böhm-Bawerk.[32]

Wicksell does no more than hint at the opportunities opened by increasing or decreasing returns. In particular, his profit theory never gets beyond the implication that positive profits exist under such conditions. The origin of such profits is not so clear, despite his proofs. And although he criticizes Walras for having "completely overlooked the significance of time in production," he seems to have done the very same thing in his own "abstract theorizing."[33]

Notes

1. For emphasis on the importance of this doctrine, see Sidney Weintraub, "Keynes and the Theory of Derived-Demand," in his *Keynes and the Monetarists* (New Brunswick, N.J.: Rutgers University Press, 1973), pp. 51–70.

2. This will be examined in Chapter 5.

3. William Stanley Jevons, *The Theory of Political Economy* (Middlesex, Eng.: Penguin Books, 1970), p. 256.

4. Ibid., p. 257.

5. Eugen von Böhm-Bawerk, *Capital and Interest*, vol. 1 (South Holland, Ill.: Libertarian Press, 1959), p. 7.

6. Though some may want to attribute some priority, at least in concept, to Antoine Augustin Cournot, *Researches into the Mathematical Principles of the Theory of Wealth* (New York: Augustus M. Kelley, 1960), esp. chaps. 11 and 12.

7. Leon Walras, *Elements of Pure Economics* (London: Allen & Unwin, 1954), p. 40.

8. Jaffé argues that Walras tried to find an actual market mechanism which would lead the economy to the equilibrium position but eventually "gave up the quest." See William Jaffé, "Another Look at Leon Walras's Theory of Tâtonnement," *History of Political Economy*, Summer 1981, p. 313.

9. Ibid., p 422.

10. When reviewing the whole from a "causal" standpoint, he leans to derived demand. See his reference to Jevons in his "Preface," ibid., pp. 44–45.

11. Ibid., p. 225.

12. Although it is doubtful whether the "normal" profits of Alfred Marshall are anything more than an attractive evasion of the zero-profits case. See Joan Robinson, *Economic Heresies* (New York: Basic Books, 1971), pp. 27–30.

13. The number of entrepreneurs is, of course, always limited by the size of the population. The relevant limit, however, is that beyond which the number of laborers becomes small enough that the now-high wages eat up profits.

14. Knut Wicksell takes this argument to its illogical conclusion; see below.

15. Walras, *Elements of Pure Economics*, p. 269.

16. See, e.g., Maurice Dobb, *Theories of Value and Distribution Since*

Adam Smith (Cambridge: Cambridge University Press, 1973), p. 205, and Robinson, *Economic Heresies*, pp. 26–27.

17. Walras, *Elements of Pure Economics*, p. 225. E. K. Hunt calls this Walrasian entrepreneur a "modern-day counterpart to the myth of Sisyphus''; see E. K. Hunt, *History of Economic Thought: A Critical Perspective* (Belmont, Calif.: Wadsworth Publishing Co., 1979), p. 290.

18. Walras, *Elements of Pure Economics*, p. 423.

19. Ibid., p. 224; emphasis added.

20. John Bates Clark, *The Distribution of Wealth* (New York: Macmillan Co., 1899). The promise appears in idem, *Essentials of Economic Theory* (New York: Macmillan Co., 1907), p. v.

21. Clark, *The Distribution of Wealth*, p. 30.

22. Actually Clark generally refers to "final" productivity, rather than "marginal" productivity. Alfred Marshall claims to adopt the word "marginal" from Thünen, though Clark's rendering of Thünen is "final." See Alfred Marshall, *Principles of Economics* (New York: Macmillan Co., 1948), p. x, and Clark, *The Distribution of Wealth*, pp. 321n.–324n.

23. Clark, *The Distribution of Wealth*, p. 79; see also pp. 201ff., 331.

24. This is the "adding-up" problem first posed by Philip Wicksteed in his *Coordination of the Laws of Distribution* (London: Macmillan & Co., 1894). Wicksteed solves the problem with a linear homogeneous production function. This draws Edgeworth's fire: "This is certainly a remarkable discovery . . . . There is a magnificence in this generalization which recalls the youth of philosophy. Justice is a perfect cube, said the ancient sage; and rational conduct is a homogeneous function, adds the modern savant." See Francis Y. Edgeworth, *Papers Relating to Political Economy*, vol. 1 (London: Macmillan & Co., 1925), p. 31.

25. Clark, *The Distribution of Wealth,* p. 321ff. To declare that each individual gets "all" that he produces involves a philosophic conundrum: all that can possibly be known is that 100 people produce X amount and 101 produce $X + \Delta X$. To say who produces what is beyond anybody's power of disentanglement. Too, when 100 or 101 people are hired *simultaneously*, there is no "last" worker.

27. Frank Knight, *Risk, Uncertainty, and Profit* (Chicago: University of Chicago Press, 1971), p. 36. See also below, Chapter 6.

28. Knut Wicksell, *Lectures on Political Economy*, vol. 1 (New York: Macmillan Co., 1934), p. 126.

29. Knut Wicksell, *Selected Papers on Economic Theory*, ed. Erik Lindahl (Cambridge: Harvard University Press, 1958), p. 96: "We could equally well have considered the workers themselves as the entrepreneurs, however."

30. Ibid., p. 98; emphasis added.

31. Wicksell, *Lectures on Political Economy*, p. 126.

32. "It was not until Böhm-Bawerk published his great work that we acquired a theory of the nature and functions of capital, and of the origin and determination of interest, which, in clearness and exhaustiveness, satisfies even the most exacting demands" (ibid., p. 147). Neither Böhm-Bawerk nor Irving Fisher is treated here; while both studied the impact of time in the economic process, the analysis was always in respect to interest on capital, and not profit.

33. Knut Wicksell, *Value, Capital, and Rent* (London: Allen & Unwin, 1954), p. 94.

CHAPTER 5

Profits and the Entrepreneur

Don't start vast projects with half-vast plans.

—Anonymous

In this new, splendid neoclassical world of marginal utilities and sovereign consumers, profits have a shadowy existence, paralleling the impotence of entrepreneurs. Where perfect foresight and/or instantaneous adjustment thrive, the entrepreneur has no special function; where everything is known, all are equal. The dissatisfaction with this conceptual state of affairs impels other neoclassical economists to rethink the role of the entrepreneur in a capitalist system. He becomes, in these schemes, neither the multifaceted businessman of classical theory nor a mere owner of capital (or land or labor). Though he may also provide alienable productive resources, he has a special function different from that, a function which gives rise to the profit income. Identifying this profit-earning function becomes the crucial task, one made more difficult by the restrictions of the general equilibrium-marginal productivity framework that continues, by and large, to occupy the center stage of economic analysis.

MARSHALL'S MANAGERIAL PROFITS

Unlike Walras, Alfred Marshall seems to have little doubt that profits are a regular feature of the economic system and as such deserve a place in distribution theory. Just what profits are, and what role they play in the economic system, however, is not so clear.

At the center of the Marshallian theory lies derived demand. "The demand schedule for any factor of production of a commodity can be *derived* from that for the commodity."[1] His well-known illustration is the demand for knife blades and knife handles being derived from the demand for knives. This apparently gives rise to the income of the productive factors.

The list of productive factors is expanded by Marshall. In the first place, distinction is made between money capital and physical capital. The former earns interest, which is positive because of the cost of "waiting," and the latter earns quasi-rent. Besides these two capitals, Marshall includes not only land and labor but also management. The latter is really composed of two parts, "business ability and energy" and "organization by which the appropriate business ability and requisite capital are brought together."[2] It is management, a productive factor, that earns profits. This is reminiscent of Mill, who considered profits partly remuneration for supervision, but is nevertheless essentially new: with Mill, profits are a residual, not a return to a factor of production.

In equilibrium, Marshall agrees, the income of the various factors of production are equal to the value of their marginal products. He declares, however, that it is an illusion to consider this a theory of distribution. "The doctrine that the earnings of a worker tend to be equal to the net product of his work, has by itself no real meaning," because it must already presuppose the rest of the economy.[3] Similarly, illustrations showing the equality of interest with the value of the marginal product of capital "cannot be made into a theory of interest . . . without reasoning in a circle."[4] This, however, contradicts his derived-demand reasoning, as does his inclusion of profits as a component part of supply price.[5] For if the value of the factors of production, including management, is derived from the value of the products they produce, then so must the incomes of the factors be derived from their productivity in this production.[6] Alternatively, if profits are to be included in the supply price of commodities, there must be an independent determination of their size (and an independent explanation of their origin). Marshall spends some time discussing the variations from the "normal" rate of profits (and the causes of these variations), but the issue of significance is the size of normal profits themselves. To this Marshall does not address himself.

He does, nonetheless, offer a justification for his categorizing of management as a productive factor. The productive power of entrepreneurs stems from their peculiar activity in production: "they 'adventure' or 'undertake' its risks; they bring together the capital and the labor required for the work; they arrange or 'engineer' its general plan, and superintend its minor detail."[7] To do this, an entrepreneur must "have a thorough knowledge of *things* in his own trade. He must have the power of forecasting the broad movement of production and consumption. . . . He must be able to judge cautiously and undertake risks boldly." In addition, "he must be a natural leader of *men*."[8]

It would seem reasonable to attempt to disentangle these various functions (more so today, when the division of labor in a large corporation is far more extensive than in Marshall's day) and examine whether profit is rightly attributed to them all or to only one (the last function—superintendence of minor details—can be safely ignored), to some managerial "group" or individual. Regarding risk, Marshall writes:

The greater part of business risks are so inseparably connected with the general management of the business that an insurance company which undertook them would really make itself responsible for the business and in consequence every firm has to act as its own insurance office with regard to them.[9]

Insofar as he views it as impossible to deal with risk as a completely insurable phenomenon—and thereby eliminate it from the examination of profit—Marshall is taking an important step toward Frank Knight and away from equilibrium; insofar, however, as he likens an enterprise to an insurance company, he omits the decisive step.

Moreover, if an enterprise is a miniature insurance company, the corresponding incomes should likewise be comparable. Unfortunately, Marshall never explains whether an insurance company's income should be considered as interest or profit, or both, or neither; consequently the analogy leads nowhere.

One thing is clear, however: he does not consider risk to be the only cause of profit. He acknowledges that its central importance in certain trades has "induced some American writers to regard profits as remuneration of risk simply; and as consisting of what remains after deducting interest and earnings of management from gross profits." This view he considers "on the whole not advantageous because it tends to class the work of management with mere routine superintendence."[10] Of course, he does this very thing himself, as indicated above. It should be noted that his failure to identify management properly leaves no room for any interpretation other than that it is "merely" a special type of labor, for he says as much: "Looking at businessmen from one point of view we may regard them as a highly skilled industrial grade" (the other point of view is that they are 'middlemen' between the manual worker and the consumer—an especially unenlightening perspective).[11]

As if wishing to drive the point home, Marshall picks this theme up in another context, saying,

There is no breach of continuity as we ascend from the unskilled laborer to the skilled, thence to the foreman, to the head of a department, to the general manager of a large business paid partly by a share of the profits, to the junior partner, and lastly to the head partner of a large private business.[12]

But on the other hand, "business undertakers are to a certain extent a class apart," and this because "it is through their conscious agency that the principle of substitution chiefly works in balancing one factor of production against another."[13] Interpreting this statement poses a problem. It seems here as though Marshall regards profits as the "cost" necessary to enforce the equilibrium rules of competition. At the same time, "the work of business management is done cheaply . . . so cheaply as to contribute to production more than the equivalent of its pay."[14] If management enforces the principle of substitution, and therefore ensures least cost, it may make the other factors of production more productive, but that hardly provides a means of measuring the productiveness of management itself. Lacking this, Marshall is left without an explanation of the origin of profits.

ROSCHER AND PIERSON: THE PROFIT WAGE

While most English economists have confounded the personal gain of the undertaker with the interest of the capital used by him, many German writers have called the "undertaker's earnings" or profit a special, and fourth, branch of the national income, co-ordinate with rent, wages, and interest on capital.[15]

In Wilhelm Roscher's own work, profits appear as something of a combination of a distinct fourth class and an outgrowth of the other three he mentions. It is testimony more to the continuing confusion regarding profit than anything else.

The entrepreneur plays a special role in Roscher's theory in that the "awakening of latent wants, a matter of utmost importance to a people who would advance in civilization, is something which can enter into the mind only of a man endowed with the spirit of enterprise (an undertaker)." The entrepreneur performs this function "by organizing and inspecting the work, calculating the chances of the whole enterprise," that is, by labor. Hence the entrepreneur's income, above and beyond rent and interest on his own land and capital, "must be considered as wages paid for his labor."[16]

Thus profits are again essentially wages for some sort of managerial or organizational labor. Hence profit "is subject essentially to the same general law as wages in general are; only it differs in this from all other branches of income, that it can never be stipulated for in advance. Rather it consists of the surplus" over and above interest, rent, and wages on common labor.[17] It is a peculiar wage, however, which is not stipulated in advance; neither is it clear why such surplus should be paid only to entrepreneurial labor.

More peculiar still is Roscher's notion that the entrepreneur receives these wages even when he doesn't perform any work, that even when he hires someone else to do the work "he earns these wages from the fact that his name keeps the whole enterprise together; and . . . he has to bear the care and responsibility attending it," for which he may have to spend "weary, watchful nights."[18] The language, and the thought, is reminiscent of Thünen. Reputation and responsibility may be important, but it is difficult to see how they could be construed as labor—at best, reputation could be considered as past labor, but then so could capital—unless insomnia is a form of labor.

The question of why this aforementioned surplus should exist, or under what conditions it would exist, remains unanswered (as does the question of what produces losses, or "negative wages"). Roscher does, however, present three determinants of the size of profits: the rarity of the undertaker's necessary qualities, the risk of the undertaking, and the disagreeableness of enterprise. Among the "necessary qualities" of the entrepreneur is "the capacity to inspire capitalists with confidence and workmen with love for their task" (the latter presumably other than by raising their wages).[19] Risk is taken here as actuarial risk; and Roscher believes that the decline over time of profits is due to the decrease of risk. As Knight argues, however, risk, as here understood, cannot lead to profits.

Nikolaas G. Pierson, who gives the theory of distribution pride of place in his exposition of economic principles, considers that "the word profit has no fixed meaning in everyday language" and that therefore any inquiry into the nature of profits must begin by clearing this up.[20] This requires understanding the nature of the entrepreneur's activity.

The entrepreneur is defined as the decision-maker, and the organizer and manager of production. He is also a borrower of capital, when that is necessary to perform these tasks. It is he, rather than the laborer, capitalist, or landowner, who is entrusted by society with this function because he has a special responsibility regarding the result: if his judgment is wrong or his decisions are incorrect, he will suffer. Therefore he incurs a special kind of risk above and beyond debtor insolvency or inability to make good on credit. The entrepreneur is also exposed to risks of this kind, but at the same time he incurs a further risk from which the other two classes of person are immune. His efforts and anxiety go for nothing, in fact they cause him damage, not only in the event of one or other of his debtors stopping payment, but also in the event of his enterprise failing to meet the wants of the community.[21]

This risk would seem to be nonactuarial, noninsurable, and Pierson therefore appears to be on the verge of making the analytical distinction between risk and Knightian uncertainty. However, he follows with remarks in a different vein, to the effect that the entrepreneur is a special type of laborer and "profit is the remuneration of this labor—the wage received by the entrepreneur for the effort and anxiety which he has undergone. . . . It forms a part of wages, if we use that word in a very wide sense."[22] If profits are nothing but a wage, then there is no trouble in locating their origin—it is the productive effort of the entrepreneur's labor—but then the entrepreneur's duties of risk-taking, organizing, decision-making, and capital-borrowing lose their essential character.

Pierson seems to oscillate from one point of view to the other. The contradiction is nowhere more evident than in his explanation—reminiscent of Roscher—that shareholders in an enterprise are receiving profits even if they do not perform any labor, for "in such cases the entrepreneurs get their labor done by other people, to whom they give a portion of the profit in the shape of wages or bonus or a combination of both."[23] Or again, "the profits made by entrepreneurs are the remuneration which they receive for their efforts, notwithstanding the fact that many entrepreneurs manage to evade these efforts."[24] It is a strain on logic to argue that the income one receives is a wage, when no labor is being rendered.

Another ambiguity regarding the entrepreneur must be noted. Although Pierson defines him by function, he does not satisfactorily explain who in the economy actually performs this function, who really corresponds to the entrepreneur of his treatise. He seems to include stockholders as profit-receivers and therefore as entrepreneurs, yet it is not obvious that they are the ones who make decisions, organize, and manage production.

Turning to profit itself, Pierson finds three distinguishable components: compensation for risk, entrepreneurs' wages "properly so-called," and surplus. Here, however, risk is not understood in the same sense as formerly, but rather as *actuarial* risk.

Everything which lessens the risks incurred by entrepreneurs will tend to diminish the total profits which accrue to them. In the days when the insurance system was less developed than now, trading with countries out of Europe was a business involving much risk . . .[25]

and therefore profits were correspondingly high. Furthermore, as risks have decreased over time, "compensation for risk does not usually amount to very much."[26] As with Marshall, the analogy to an insurance company seems to obscure and confuse matters more than to clarify them.

The element that constitutes entrepreneurs' wages—the "chief element in most profits"—is determined like any other wage, namely, by supply and demand.[27] The latter is determined by the size of the population, the material welfare of the population, the amount of exportable goods a country produces, and the size of enterprise. The first three factors are concerned with demand for goods in general (inadequately treated), while the fourth is a mediating one relating demand for goods in general to demand for entrepreneurs—that is, given the level of aggregate demand, the greater the size of a typical enterprise, the fewer entrepreneurs will be needed to meet that demand. The supply of entrepreneurial services depends solely on the wages that would-be entrepreneurs could make if they worked for someone else rather than as entrepreneurs.

This is a curious argument, on two counts. In the first place, it is only a partial analysis, for it leaves unexamined the rate of wages for workers other than entrepreneurs. And since the argument could easily be turned around to make the general supply of labor, or rate of wages, depend on the entrepreneurs' wages, it is circular (he does not claim mutual determination). In the second place, the logical comparison would be not between the general rate of wages and entrepreneurs' wages as a component of profits but between the general rate of wages and the *total profits* (at the very least, entrepreneurs' wages and surplus). Whenever the latter is greater than the former, the number of entrepreneurs could be expected to increase, regardless of how much of profits is made up of the wages element.

The third element of profit—surplus—is simply the difference between what the least favorably situated entrepreneur earns vis-à-vis the more favorably situated entrepreneurs—a variation on Ricardo's differential rent—applied to entrepreneurs. The more advantageous position results from a good reputation from long-established practices, a large capital, good business connections, easy credit, monopoly, and better information. These are all factors inhibiting perfect competition as generally understood. Pierson states quite clearly that these factors are always operating, and there is never a situation where no entrepreneurs receive a surplus.

SCHUMPETER: INNOVATION AND PROFITS

Alluding to Clark, "whose theory is nearest to mine," Joseph Schumpeter views profits as a phenomenon only of a dynamic economy.[28] The elaboration of what exactly is entailed therein, however, is much advanced over Clark.

In Schumpeter's static economy, which he refers to as the "circular flow" of economic life, "production must flow on essentially profitless."[29] By now-familiar reasoning, competition succeeds in eliminating profits entirely by dispersing them among the original productive factors (reduced to two—land and labor—capital being an entirely different substance).[30] He goes even further, stating that in this circular flow, the entrepreneur "has no function of a special kind there, he simply does not exist."[31]

"That the economic system in its most perfect condition should operate without profit is a paradox" that, however, vanishes by understanding that "as value is a symptom of our poverty, so profit is a symptom of imperfection."[32] This "imperfection" is the dynamic state of the economy, which Schumpeter calls economic development and which is the actual state of any economy. In fact, to cling to the "fiction" of the circular flow "is to hide an essential thing which . . . is theoretically important and the source of the explanation of phenomena which would not exist without it."[33]

In contrast to the conditions of circular flow, which may be described as an "adaptation to data existing at any time," development results from "spontaneous changes in the data with which the individual is accustomed to reckon."[34] That means "such changes in economic life as are not forced upon it from without but arise by its own initiative."[35] For this reason, Schumpeter excludes changes in tastes or wants, since these lie outside the scope of economics. He also excludes "mere growth of the economy"—growth, that is, of population or capital, as "it calls forth no qualitatively new phenomena" and is therefore analogous to external change.[36] Thus, Schumpeter is not interested in presenting the economy as merely an equilibrating mechanism, changing only through external shocks, but which if left to itself would produce a permanent state of general equilibrium. Instead, he seeks internal forces of development, and in this respect his approach is "more nearly parallel to Marx" than to the other neoclassical writers.[37]

Schumpeter identifies five types of change which produce economic development: introduction of new goods, new methods of production, opening of new markets, conquest of new sources of raw materials, and introduction of new organization (including, for example, monopolization). All five have in common that they act to combine materials and forces in new ways; alternatively, "development in our sense is then defined by the carrying out of new combinations."[38]

It is the entrepreneur whose role it is to bring about such new combinations by innovation, though not necessarily to invent them, for Schumpeter distinguishes the two: invention is the source of knowledge, innovation is the application. In order to do so, he must remove some of the means of production from their old combinations; this he does by means of credit. The creation of *new purchasing power* which is credited to entrepreneurs is in fact the function of capital.[39] Because the new purchasing power out of expanded bank credit comes into existence before new values, there is an inflation; indeed, this inflationary process is the means by which the entrepreneur gains control of means of production. The rise in prices, however, is only temporary.[40]

Now "entrepreneurial profit is a surplus over costs" which, of course, is nonexistent in the circular flow.[41] By new combinations, which produce more for less, a surplus is created so long as three counter-conditions are overcome, namely, the tendency for a fall in the price of the product due to greater supply, the tendency for prices of production goods to increase as a result of greater demand, and the costs of the new combinations themselves. These have been overcome "in-numerable times in practice. This proves the possibility of surplus over costs," that is, of profits.[42] Summarizing, he says, "Without development there is no profit, without profit no development."[43]

Schumpeter makes it clear that his theory has nothing in common with the theory that profit is a return to risk. In fact, "the entrepreneur is never the risk-bearer." The entrepreneur, as entrepreneur, has nothing to lose (save his reputation, which apparently is not worth much); the risk falls on the creditor. "Risk-taking is in no case an element of the entrepreneurial function."[44]

However, "new businesses are continually arising under the impulse of the alluring profit." This entrepreneur soon runs into competitors, "who first reduce and then *annihilate his profit*."[45] Industry is reorganized, and a new equilibrium position results from the new data, with the prices of products once again equaling costs; consequently "the surplus of the entrepreneur in question and of his immediate followers disappears."[46] What first appeared as profit is now transformed into wages and rents, and the circular flow runs once again on its invariant course.

By connecting profit not with invention as such, but rather with its introduction, Schumpeter escapes Knight's criticism of Clark that change, if foreseen, cannot produce profit, for the introduction of new combinations is necessarily unknown, at least in part, else it would be done generally and therefore would not be a specific function of the entrepreneur. If there is a problem here, it lies more in being able to distinguish between scientific invention and commercial marketing of the invention. Furthermore, patents (or simply monopoly) could have the effect of transferring the surplus over costs not to the entrepreneur, who introduces or applies an invention, but to the inventor—in which case the surplus is no longer a profit.

On the other hand, Schumpeter still clings to the view that the economy, the changing economy, is simply a succession of changeless ones; the dynamic economy is nothing more than the continual disruption of equilibrium—and therefore continual appearance of profits—followed however by the tendency to return to equilibrium. His intention to present the economy as one which develops on its own is only partially realized. It is true that by identifying change as residing within the process of enterprise (whose moving force is the entrepreneur), Schumpeter goes beyond the notion that the economy is simply a Clarkian equilibrium responding to occasional external disturbances. Nevertheless, the conception of profit as something the economy continually "annihilates," something which is forever slipping from the entrepreneur's grasp, is one which has not yet entirely overcome the neoclassical equilibrium influence.

HAWLEY AND THE RISK THEORY

Frederick B. Hawley is the leading proponent of what he describes as the "risk theory of profit." He takes other writers to task not only for not recognizing the true role of risk in profits but also for important failures in assessing the entrepreneur and his activity and importance in the economic world. Indeed, for Hawley the entrepreneur is the *key* element of the productive process, and profit is the *key* income in the economic system. Any "learned" treatises that purport to deal with the distribution of wealth and fail to notice profits receive his disdain. Böhm-Bawerk's lengthy *Capital and Interest* is, in Hawley's eyes, founded on the fundamental error of disregarding the entrepreneur entirely.

It seems to me that the industrial function of the undertaker, the consideration of which is thus unceremoniously brushed aside, must first be understood before the problem of interest can be attacked at all. . . . Great divergence of view exists, indeed, as to what the industrial functions of the undertaker are. But, unless it can be shown that the employment of capital in production is not among them, it would surely seem the natural course to pursue, in attacking the problem of interest, to find out why the undertaker is willing to pay interest on the capital.[47]

This great flaw in economic theory is not eliminated, says Hawley, by those who make profits a return to the activity of coordination of the productive process. In the first place, coordination is not a well-defined concept; it must include the planning of activity, as well as the actual carrying-out of the activity, so that both the planner and the "executant," two different people, must be considered as coordinators. Furthermore, coordination, "whether we regard it as managing, selecting, or planning, is an act of mental labor . . . and if profit is its reward, profits are either a kind of wages, or labor earns two entirely distinct kinds of reward."[48] It should be noted that Hawley is clearly not talking about a stationary flow where coordination only has to be performed once.

Instead, what is significant about the entrepreneur is that he takes responsibility, and therefore risk, for the production process, for the actual carrying-out of production. Someone must take responsibility for this, otherwise it would not get done. In this sense, "enterprise is the source of all economic activity."[49] And the "enterprise," in assuming responsibility and risk over production, acquires ownership of the product. Wages, rent, and interest are paid "not with any share of the product itself, but with stipulated amounts of purchasing power"—that is, in predetermined amounts.[50] Beyond this, a positive net income results, which is *unpredetermined* and which belongs to the entrepreneur. This net income is profit.

Hawley is speaking not only of actuarial risk, or risk which can be perfectly insured against. Such risk would not be an unpredetermined income; anyway, "no one, as a matter of business, subjects himself to risk for what he believes the actuarial value of the risk amounts to."[51]

Confusion nevertheless remains: "To the extent in which he insures, he restricts his exercise of his function, but the risk is merely transferred to the insurer, who becomes himself an enterpriser and the recipient of an unpredetermined income."[52] Further, the enterpriser "renders to each class a service similar to an assurance company."[53] Again, the analogy to an insurance company is inappropriate, since there is no discussion of how such an enterprise, if indeed it is an enterprise in Hawley's sense, obtains a net return. In fact, if risk-taking is the essential function of enterprise, an examination of an insurance company would presumably be the clearest means of illustrating the principles on which this theory of profits is maintained. The difference between risk which can and uncertainty which cannot be perfectly insured against (to use Knight's terms) is nowhere examined. Indeed, risk and the causes of risk are nowhere diagnosed.

One result is that Hawley can provide no clear, direct confirmation that profits are on the whole positive rather than zero (or even negative). Indeed, he remarks at one point,

the entrepreneur exacts, first, compensation for the average loss which is to be expected, and secondly an additional gain as the reward of his assumption of the uncertainty as to how each individual transaction will turn out. In the long run, losses and gains due to price fluctuations . . . tend to balance out

so that aggregate profits would appear to be zero, although "uncertainty as to how price fluctuations will affect each individual transaction remains," as do, therefore, individual profits and losses.[54] Elsewhere, however, he argues that entrepreneurs who are making losses or zero-profits are constantly disappearing, indeed, "the fact of their being persistent losers is evidence that they are in the process of elimination."[55] That would appear to leave only the profitable producers in existence, and therefore on balance positive profits.

This would be at least conceivable if the number of entrepreneurs were limited—relative to the size of the population. This is, in fact, the model adopted by Hawley. The special function of enterprise, the motive force of the economy which "stands on a different footing from, and above, the other productive factors" and which "alone is productive," is assumed by a "distinct class of individuals."[56] To Hawley it is not open to everyone to be an entrepreneur; rather, only certain individuals are in this class (whose cause Hawley champions as much as the classical economists did that of the classical entrepreneur). This limitation on membership in the entrepreneurial class, however, may be enough to explain why profits would not be dissipated by competition; but it would certainly not suggest any cause for their appearing at all (unless the limitation is severe enough to produce monopoly-like returns). This remains a gap in Hawley's theory.

Hawley does respond to those who, like Schumpeter, argue that risks in production are borne by the capitalist, the owner of capital, rather than the entrepreneur, who is merely a borrower and therefore stands to lose only other people's wealth. The entrepreneur does indeed borrow capital (which is defined by Hawley as a claim to material wealth), but with that capital he *buys*, and therefore *owns*, capital goods, which he stands to lose. Moreover, the entrepreneur is the owner of the product and, in a sense, of all material wealth involved in production; all this he risks by actually undertaking to produce (this is in some ways reminiscent of the wage-fund doctrine).

What Hawley doesn't clear up is who exactly he considers to be an enterpriser. The function of enterprise, of taking responsibility and risk, is clear enough, but to whom does this function fall, for example, in a modern corporation—to the board of directors? to the stockholders? The latter can hardly be assigned the task of undertaking production, but it is even more obscure to assign to the former the onerous task of absorbing risks. Since Hawley himself criticizes other economists who "have not . . . defined profit in terms of the entrepreneur because they have not yet succeeded in formulating any satisfactory concept of either," these deficiencies are all the more puzzling.[57] While Hawley might be commended in his rebuke of those who have left this hole in economic theory, he has nevertheless not succeeded in closing the gap himself.

NEOCLASSICAL THEORY: PROFIT FACTORS AND EQUILIBRIUM

It can hardly be said that neoclassical theory manages to solve the profit problem; indeed, if anything, it exacerbates it. The pervasive influence of equilibrium theory and marginal productivity theory—cornerstones of the new analysis—prevent any meaningful profit theory from emerging. In such a setting, only two alternatives for profit exist: profit survives in the interstices of equilibrium—that is, in the disequilibrium before the calm and the "imperfections" of monopoly—or profit must be the return to some factor analogous to rent from land. The former is the basis for Walras's assertion that profits are exceptional, not normal, and leads to the abandonment of profit theory. The latter leads to attempts to locate in the entrepreneurial function a special productive factor that earns as its reward profit. But in this conception, either enterprise is rewarded for the work accomplished—in which case profits are indistiguishable from wages—or enterprise is rewarded regardless of work accomplished—in which case it is merely deceptive to call them a productive "reward." Furthermore, there is no room here for any residual income, and hence, no room for uncertainty, but it is precisely in the world of perfect certainty that the entrepreneur's special function disappears entirely.[58]

This is implicitly recognized by some. Schumpeter's theory of development and Hawley's risk theory are examples of economists trying to escape the equilibrium-marginal productivity straightjacket. The former's emphasis on dynamic changes, occurring within the economy, and the latter's inkling that the certainty of economic models is an inaccurate reflection of the economy itself both point to alternative approaches that can be more fruitful in understanding profits. The power of entrenched ideas, however, prevents them from making the full break necessary. As a result, profit theory advances little.

Notes

1. Alfred Marshall, *Principles of Economics* (New York: Macmillan Co., 1948), p. 383.
2. Ibid., p. 313.
3. Ibid., p. 518.
4. Ibid., p. 519; see also p. 410.
5. Ibid., p. 343.
6. Strictly speaking, it is only the demand, not the value, that Marshall sees as derived. But since the supply of management—the second of the two "blades of a scissors"—is nowhere to be found in Marshall, the derivation must hold for value as well.
7. Ibid., p. 243.
8. Ibid., p. 297.
9. Ibid., p. 398.
10. Ibid., pp. 612–13.
11. Ibid., p. 293.
12. Ibid., p. 663.
13. Ibid.
14. Ibid., p. 664. He also suggests that the "robber barons" gave back more, in the form of economies, than they "robbed" (ibid., p. 686).
15. Wilhelm Roscher, *Principles of Political Economy* (New York: Henry Holt, 1878), vol. 2, p. 146. "Undertaker" is a literal translation of the German *Unternehmer*, or entrepreneur.
16. Ibid., p. 147.
17. Ibid., p. 148.
18. Ibid.
19. Ibid., p. 149.
20. Nikolaas G. Pierson, *Principles of Economics* (London: Macmillan & Co., 1902), vol. 1, p. 233. "Marx upside down"; see their
21. Ibid., p. 235.
22. Ibid., p. 236.
23. Ibid.
24. Ibid., p. 237.
25. Ibid., p. 240.

26. Ibid., p. 241.
27. Ibid.
28. Joseph Schumpeter, *The Theory of Economic Development*, Harvard Economic Studies, vol. 46 (Cambridge: Harvard University Press, 1961), p. 128n.
29. Ibid., p. 31.
30. In this he too follows Böhm-Bawerk, his teacher.
31. Nicholas Kaldor later concludes that a firm has significance only in a dynamic economy, and "is only required so long as adjustments are required. . . . It is essentially a feature not of 'equilibrium' but of 'disequilibrium'; it is needed only so long as . . . the actual situation . . . deviates from the equilibrium situation." See his "The Equilibrium of the Firm," *Economic Journal*, March 1934, p. 70.
32. Schumpeter, *Theory of Economic Development*, p. 31.
33. Ibid., p. 80.
34. Ibid., p. 62.
35. Ibid., pp. 33, 62.
36. Ibid., p. 63.
37. Ibid., p. 60n. Joan Robinson and John Eatwell refer to his theory as "Marx upside down "; see their *Introduction to Modern Economics* (London: McGraw-Hill Book Co., 1973), p. 46.
38. Schumpeter, *Theory of Economic Development*, p. 66.
39. Capital "is a fund of purchasing power" (ibid., p. 120) or "capital is nothing but the lever by which the entrepreneur subjects to his control the concrete goods which he needs, nothing but a means of diverting the factors of production to new uses" (ibid., p. 116).
40. Ibid., pp. 108–112.
41. Ibid., p. 128.
42. Ibid., p. 131. This is both gratuitous and unnecessary. The existence of profits "proves" their possibility without any theorizing at all.
43. Ibid., p. 154.
44. Ibid., p. 137.
45. Ibid., p. 89; emphasis added.
46. Ibid., pp. 131–32.
47. Frederick B. Hawley, "The Fundamental Error of 'Kapital und Kapitalzins,' " *Quarterly Journal of Economics*, April 1892, p. 281.
48. Frederick B. Hawley, *Enterprise and the Productive Process* (New York: Knickerbocker Press, 1907), p. 110.
49. Ibid., p. 94.
50. Ibid., p. 62.
51. Ibid., p. 106.
52. Ibid., p. 111.
53. Hawley, "The Fundamental Error of 'Kapital und Kapitalzins,' " p. 283.
54. Frederick B. Hawley, "Reply to Final Objections to the Risk Theory of Profit," *Quarterly Journal of Economics*, August 1901, pp. 603–4.
55. Frederick B. Hawley "Profits and the Residual Theory," *Quarterly Journal of Economics*, July 1890, p. 389.
56. Hawley, *Enterprise and the Productive Process*, pp. 112, 95.
57. Ibid., p. 165.

58. Schumpeter, *Theory of Economic Development*, p. 76, and Nicolas Kaldor, *Essays in Value and Distribution* (Glencoe, Ill.: Free Press, 1960), p. 70.

CHAPTER 6

Profits and Uncertainty

I accuse the classical [neoclassical] economic theory of being itself one of those pretty, polite techniques which tries to deal with the present by abstracting from the fact that we know very little about the future.
                                                                —*John Maynard Keynes*

The work done in economic theory after the emergence of neoclassical equilibrium and marginal productivity—which removed profits from the main line of inquiry and analysis—thus produced pieces of, and indicated directions for, profit theory, but did not resolve the difficulty. Frank Knight draws on these pieces and directions and alters this unsatisfactory state. While prefacing his book with the note that it contains little new—"its object is refinement, not reconstruction"—Knight nevertheless imparts a consistent profit framework to neoclassical theory.[1]

Knight clearly construes the nature of the profit income as one of the central issues for economic analysis. He opens his book by pronouncing that "the problem of profit is one way of looking at the problem of the contrast between perfect competition and actual competition," since it is the attribute of the former to "tend" to eliminate profits, while the latter continually records profits (or losses).[2] Or again, it is the existence or absence of profits "which is the essential distinction between theoretical and actual economic society," where by "theoretical economic society" is meant the general equilibrium model of perfect competition.[3] It is odd that Knight continues to refer to economic theory as the economics of general equilibrium, in contrast to the conclusions of his own work, so that he later remarks that "a theory of profit is inherently a theory of *aberrations* of actual economic conditions from the theoretical consequences or tendencies of the more general price forces which tend to eliminate them," and that profit is "the difference between any income as it actually is and what it would be in the theoretical position of general equilibrium."[4] In this he assigns to equilibrium theory more than its due—by seeming to deny to the theory of profits a place in the corpus of economic theory. Overlooking this timidity, it is beyond doubt that the issue of profits is fundamental for Knight.

Knight defines profit simply enough, namely, as the difference between cost and selling price (this, at least, is "pure" profit). Alternatively, profit is the lone genuine residual income, all other incomes being "contractual income, which is essentially *rent*."[5] While such pure profit is never found, and impossible to measure, he nevertheless finds it capable of being analyzed. Before doing so, however, Knight introduces the notion of *uncertainty*, the central factor in creating the profit income. Indeed, he believes that the pervasiveness of uncertainty is "the most important underlying difference between the conditions which theory is compelled to assume and those which exist in fact."[6] Hence his preliminary elaboration of the concept.

UNCERTAINTY VERSUS RISK

Uncertainty differs from risk in the usual sense (actuarial risk); the latter is connected with mathematical probability. Knight defines risk as the "empirical evaluation of the frequency of association between predicates, not analyzable into varying combinations of equally probable alternatives."[7] Risk has the important property of being measurable in advance of the activity to which it is subject. Such a risk, however, presents the producer with no real uncertainty in his operations. Because it is measurable in advance, the risk will operate, given the opportunity for the "law of large numbers" to play a role, as a known or predictable cost. The principle is no different from the prediction of how many heads will result from tossing a coin one thousand times. Knight writes as follows:

If in a certain class of cases a given outcome is not certain, nor even extremely probable, but only contingent, but if the numerical probability of its occurrence is known, conduct in relation to the situation in question may be ordered intelligently. . . .

Thus, in the example given by von Mangoldt, the bursting of bottles does not introduce any uncertainty or hazard into the business of producing champagne; since in the operations of any producer a practically constant and known proportion of the bottles burst, it does not especially matter even whether the proportion is large or small. The loss becomes a fixed cost in the industry and is passed on to the consumer, like the outlays for labor or materials or any other.[8]

Because such risk is easily subsumed as a "fixed" cost (fixed, that is, in the above example, for a given number of champagne bottles; i.e., a variable cost is contemporary terminology), there is no real uncertainty. In fact, there is no reason to consider production under conditions of *risk* any different from production under conditions of *complete certainty*, there being nothing essentially to distinguish them. Hence there is no occasion for the emergence of profit; this special class of income is a residual from selling price after costs are deducted, and risk is deducted as part of the costs.

THE HAWLEY CRITICISM

The distinction between risk and uncertainty forms the basis of Knight's criticism of the risk theorists, especially Hawley.

He [Hawley] and his opponents alike have failed to appreciate the fundamental difference between a determinate uncertainty or risk and an indeterminate, unmeasurable one. . . . If risk were exclusively of the nature of a known chance or mathematical probability, there could be no reward of risk-taking; the fact of risk could exert no influence on the distribution of income in any way.[9]

Emphasizing his basic point regarding risk, Knight says that "there is a fundamental distinction between the reward for taking a known risk and that for assuming a risk whose value itself is not known. It is so fundamental indeed, that . . . a known risk will not lead to any reward or special payment at all."[10]

It is possible, of course, that although a risk is known the individual producer does not deal with a sufficiently large set of outcomes to be assured of the results. This still fails, however, to obscure the distinction made, as the problem admits of an easy solution, namely,

. . . an organization taking in a large number of producers. This, of course, is the principle of insurance. . . . The effect is to . . . cover the operations of a large number of persons and convert the contingency into a fixed cost. It makes no difference in the principles whether the grouping of cases is effected through a mutual organization of the persons directly affected or through an outside commercial agency.[11]

Knight briefly sums up the nature of the income of an insurance agency. "Under competitive conditions and assuming that the probabilities involved are accurately known, an . . . insurer will make no clear profit and the premiums will . . . be equal to the administrative costs of carrying on the business."[12] This too is a criticism intended for Hawley, who believed that to the degree that a producer covered his risks by insurance, he transferred the profits of the enterprise to the insurer.

Knight points out that the principle of insurance is the same "whether the persons liable to a given contingency organize among themselves into a fraternal or mutual society or whether they separately contract with an outside party to bear their losses."[13] He could have added that the same principle is in effect in speculation. Through the operations of future markets and arbitrage, the producer can shift his risk to the market itself, regardless of whether this involves large-scale speculators who are doing, in effect, the job of insurers, or individuals, each of whom may be, in fact, gambling, but the sum of whom act, for the producers, as an insurer.

THE IMPACT OF UNCERTAINTY

In contrast to risk, in this sense, is uncertainty. This true uncertainty means insufficient knowledge of the outcome of an event to make even a probability estimate; true uncertainty allows no possibility of determining the outcome in advance regardless of the number of cases considered. Uncertainty, therefore, is *unknown* "risk," or *unmeasurable* "risk"; that is, it is genuine lack of knowledge regarding the future, genuine indeterminateness. It is precisely this unmeasurable "risk" or true uncertainty that Knight sees as the basic missing element in general equilibrium theory, or, rather, the distinguishing feature between the theory and the facts.[14]

Just how important uncertainty is in real economic (indeed, in all social) activity, Knight makes abundantly clear. Without uncertainty there would be hardly any economics as it is now understood. "With uncertainty entirely absent, every individual being in possession of perfect knowledge of the situation, there would be no occasion for anything of the nature of responsible management or control of productive activity [or] marketing operations."[15] Nor would there be any real point in studying economic activity, since the future being known, and therefore not problematical, economics would shed no meaningful analytical light on the subject. Indeed, the same would be true of all science, all branches of knowledge. Knight believes that "with uncertainty absent . . . it seems likely that all organic adjustments would become mechanical, all organisms automata."[16] The indubitable presence of uncertainty—and the corresponding development of intelligent thought—obviously does not preclude the assumption, for the purposes of analysis, of an economy of certainty; but Knight's point can only be interpreted as sharp criticism of analysis that does not proceed beyond that assumption.[17]

Knight also presents the problem in other, albeit similar, words—namely, that "the existence of a problem of knowledge depends on the future being different from the past, while the possibility of the solution of the problem depends on the future being like the past."[18] This probably overstates the link between present and past solutions, but nevertheless serves to illustrate

Knight's point that the problem of uncertainty is inevitably connected with that of *time*.

> At the bottom of the uncertainty problem in economics is the forward-looking character of the economic process itself. Goods are produced to satisfy wants; the production of goods requires time, and two elements of uncertainty are introduced. . . . First, the end of productive operations must be estimated from the beginning. It is notoriously impossible to tell accurately when entering upon productive activity what will be its results in physical terms, what (a) quantities and (b) qualities of goods will result from the expenditure of given resources. Second, the wants which the goods are to satisfy are also, of course, in the future to the same extent, and their prediction involves uncertainty in the same way. The producer, then, must estimate (1) the future demand which he is striving to satisfy and (2) the future results of his operations in attempting to satisfy that demand.[19]

To the modern reader there is nothing startling in this, of course—however much it might be overlooked in a host of theoretical models: if production took no time at all, knowledge of today's wants would eliminate demand uncertainty; and the instantaneous character of the production process would permit instantaneous correction of any deficiencies that might result from quantity or quality errors, thus eliminating supply uncertainty. Knight is simply taking pains to expose all underlying assumptions.

Facing uncertainty, and the time-consuming process of production, the producer has certain special tasks. In particular, "the producer takes the responsibility for forecasting consumers' wants."[20] This forecasting is necessarily imperfect, but Knight points out that it is perhaps not quite so impossible as it might seem at first sight, for while the future effective demand of an individual consumer might well be almost impossible to predict, even for the consumer himself, there is some stability to effective demand for consumers as a whole. This he attributes to the law of large numbers.[21] Even so, however, men are not equally capable of dealing with this uncertainty, and for several reasons.

> (1) Men differ in their capacity to *form correct judgments* as to the future course of events in the environment. . . . (2) Another . . . difference is found in men's capacities to *judge means* and discern and plan the steps and adjustments necessary to meet the anticipated future situation. (3) There is a variation in the power to *execute* the plans and adjustments believed to be requisite and desirable. (4) . . . there is diversity in conduct

. . . due to differences in the amount of confidence which individuals feel in their judgments when formed and in their powers of execution. . . . (5) Distinct from confidence felt is the *conative attitude* to a situation.[22]

The origin of these differences does not concern Knight, but the consequence of them he detects to be enormous. There results a natural specialization of work, according to ability to deal with uncertainty. In particular, some individuals assume responsibility for production— become producers—while the remaining individuals do not; that is, there results the "*enterprise and wage system of industry*. Its existence in the world is a direct result of the fact of uncertainty." Enterprise, for Knight, means "the *responsible direction* of economic life, the neglected feature of which is the inseparability of . . . *responsibility and control*."[23] It is the producer— the person who controls production—who is responsible for the results of production. Thus, the producer, or, better, the entrepreneur, is fundamentally different from a mere manager, who, whatever control he may exercise, assumes no responsibility. In a world of certainty the notion of responsibility would have no operative meaning, and therefore there could be no entrepreneurs. "When, however, the managerial function comes to require the exercise of judgment involving *liability to error*," that is, when uncertainty is present, "the manager becomes an entrepreneur." Of course, not every manager becomes an entrepreneur, but only he who, in addition to performing the "old mechanical routine functions . . . also makes responsible decisions."[24]

The same process also brings into existence a wholly new class of income claimants. The manager earns a wage, but the income of the entrepreneur "will normally contain in addition to wages a pure differential element designated as 'profit' by the economic theorist."[25] There are now "*two kinds of income* . . . contractual income, which is essentially *rent*, as economic theory describes incomes, and residual income, or profit."[26]

CONTRACTUAL INCOME

Knight does not mean to suggest that there are no differences between wages, interest, and rent proper, but he does seek to establish that they are fundamentally alike when compared with profit, the latter being a genuinely unique income. The former are all definite incomes received for productive services to be rendered; profit is nothing of the sort, but rather simply the surplus (possibly negative) that remains of the value of production over and above the incomes paid for productive services. Or, as Knight says elsewhere, profit is "undetermined" income: "the entrepreneur's income is not determined at all; it is 'what is left' after the others are determined."[27] It remains for Knight to show that such an income really exists as a normal feature of the economy.

The contractual incomes are all settled in the market for productive services.

Assuming perfect competition in the market for productive services, the contractual incomes are fixed for every entrepreneur by the competitive or marginal anticipations of entrepreneurs as a group in relation to the supply of each kind of agency in existence.[28]

As far as the entrepreneur is concerned, the supply of the productive factors may be taken as given. The demand for factors depends, first, on the number of entrepreneurs. Any individual can become an entrepreneur; all he need do is enter the market for productive services, buying those he needs, then directing the production process (or hiring someone to do so), and selling the product. Whether a given individual will, in fact, become an entrepreneur depends on whether he believes he can make a profit doing so; that is, it depends on "his believing (strongly enough to act upon the conviction) that he can make productive services yield more than the price fixed upon them by what other persons think they can make them yield (with the same provision that the belief must lead to action)."[29] Or, to put it differently, the market works in this way:

The laborer asks what he thinks the entrepreneur will be able to pay, and in any case will not accept less than he can get from some other entrepreneur, or by turning entrepreneur himself. In the same way the entrepreneur offers to any laborer what he thinks he must in order to secure his services, and in any case not more than he thinks the laborer will be worth to him, keeping in mind what he can get by turning laborer himself.[30]

These various offers and acceptances would all come to the same level if there were no uncertainty; in that case, everyone would know the effect of his productive services, and therefore the true value of these services *after* production and sale. No discrepancy could arise (nor, it would seem, would there be any function for the market to perform). But, in fact, there is uncertainty. And "the main uncertainty which affects the entrepreneurs is that connected with the sale price of his product."[31] Obviously, if that were known it would be possible to calculate the realized values of all productive services and compare them with the market prices for these services. But uncertainty and the time-consuming process of production require that both the owners of these services and the entrepreneurs *estimate* these *beforehand*. The payoffs thus depend on current anticipations; this is the crucial point.

PROFIT ORIGIN

For a particular entrepreneur, then, profit is a result of his being able to produce (and sell) a value that is greater than the aggregate contractual costs incurred for productive services. This requires that two conditions be met. First, the owners of the productive services must in general *underestimate* the value of the services; for if they correctly estimate their future worth, or even overestimate it, they would turn entrepreneur themselves rather than sell the services at too low a price. This would, of course, drive product prices down (and costs of productive services up), eating up profits. Second, the competition among entrepreneurs must *not* drive the prices of productive services up to, or beyond, the point of their actual future worth—and this regardless of their owners' estimations. That is, entrepreneurs in general must not overestimate their own ability to produce and realize a value. Since, again, anyone may become an entrepreneur, this second condition dovetails with the first. Knight expresses it this way:

The income of *any particular entrepreneur* will in general tend to be larger: (1) as he himself has ability, and good luck; but (2) perhaps more important, as there is in society a scarcity of self-confidence combined with the power to make effective guarantees to employees. The abundance or scarcity of mere ability to manage business successfully exerts relatively little influence on profit; the main thing is the rashness or timidity of entrepreneurs (actual and potential) as a class in bidding up the price of productive services.[32]

In regard to the latter point, it follows that abundance of business ability is genuinely advantageous to society in the aggregate, even if the entrepreneurs with such ability are not necessarily specially rewarded.

The profits of the individual entrepreneur are therefore closely tied to the fortunes of entrepreneurs as a whole. It is indeed possible (Knight thinks it likely) that aggregate profits will be negative.

This would be the natural result in a population combining low ability with high "courage." On the other hand, if men generally judge their own abilities well, the *general rate* of profit will probably be low, whether ability itself is high or low. . . . The condition for large profits is a narrowly limited supply of high-grade ability with a low general level of initiative as well as ability.

Or, as Knight explains elsewhere, the condition for positive aggregate profits is that entrepreneurs "*underestimate* the prospects of their business relatively to their dispositions to venture."[33] This comes to much the same thing. Knight does not raise the specter of lack of competition among entrepreneurs, whether due to supra-market conditions or to barriers to perfect entry into the field of entrepreneurship. Either would tend to increase profits.

Knight's theory of profits seems to have this in common with most other neoclassical theories: that profit is in some sense "taken" from the value produced by the productive factors, and hence is the difference between what the productive factors are paid and the value their services actually produce. However, with Knight, there is no tendency for this to disappear in the face of competition (though there is also no tendency for profits to remain at any given level). Uncertainty is the operative condition, and it is always present (even when conditions are not changing); hence profit (or loss) is continually being produced.[34]

ENTREPRENEURS

The actual measurement of profit is impossible, however, because it is inextricably bound up with other incomes for the entrepreneur. "In no case is it possible to determine objectively and accurately the amount of the profit element in an income, since this would involve an accurate determination of every detail of the position of equilibrium."[35]

Typically, the entrepreneur's income includes "the ordinary wage for the routine services of labor,"[36] though "the discussion of profit in relation to wages of management has been greatly over-worked. The connection with property income is enormously more common, direct, and close."[37] The entrepreneur's income, that is, includes, besides profit, both rent and interest in the usual senses, as well as wages. Conversely, property-owners typically bear uncertainty and hence earn profit. Therefore it becomes problematical who in reality exercises the entrepreneurial function, who really is earning a profit. "Pure" entrepreneurs may not exist; yet entrepreneurs must exist, otherwise the theory has no significance.

How can these entrepreneurs be identified? Knight explains that the entrepreneur has the "peculiar twofold function of (a) exercising responsible control and (b) securing the owners of productive services against uncertainty and fluctuation in their incomes, which may be summed up simply as uncertainty-bearing."[38] The task for economists, then, is to identify the bearers of uncertainty in the modern world.

Although everyone faces uncertainty, in one sense or another, not everyone bears uncertainty in the sense Knight intends. He illustrates with the example of a modern corporation, beginning

at the very "bottom" of the scale, with the "routine" duties of the common, unskilled laborer. . . . Even the coarsest and most mechanical labor involves in some sense meeting uncertainty, dealing with contingencies which cannot be *exactly* foreseen.

All human labor involves a degree of thought; "*purely* routine operations are inevitably taken over by machines." Therefore the laborer's task will "practically always be found to require conscious judgment, which is to say the meeting of uncertainty, the exercise of responsibility in the ordinary sense of these terms." Nevertheless,

the work of the common laborer does not involve uncertainty or responsibility in the effective sense. . . . Even when it is impossible to reduce the work itself to routine . . . it is possible to judge with a high degree of accuracy the capacity of a human individual to deal with the sort of irregularities to be met with in the occupation. It is the function of the operative in industry to deal with uncertainty as a matter of routine! [39]

That is, the laborer is responsible for doing the work, but the corporate managers hold the *foreman* responsible for *selecting* laborers who can meet the performance standards—including handling uncertainty as it appears in their work.

The same is true at the next level, and at every level of the corporate structure. Each individual is responsible to his superior, to whom he therefore passes on the responsibility for meeting uncertainty. Knight remarks that "what we call 'control' consists mainly of selecting someone else to do the 'controlling.' Business judgment is chiefly judgment of men." [40]

Yet the corporation as a whole bears responsibility and uncertainty with regard to the economy as a whole—the "outside world"— and someone must be the ultimate "bearer" for the corporation, or else profits would be received without being earned. Knight's answer, however, is not as neat or as simple as the question. There is, says Knight,

a complicated division or diffusion of entrepreneurship, distributed in the typical modern organization by a hierarchy of security issues carrying every conceivable gradation and combination of rights to control and to freedom from uncertainty as to income and vested capital.

This means that

the owner of resources is taking a certain share of responsibility or risk, obviously . . . he is also exercising control. . . . Control is completely absent from the function of furnishing productive services to a business only in case an accurately determined competitive value of the services is effectively guaranteed.

And in this sense, "the distinction between stocks and bonds begins to fade out."[41]

On the other hand, the board of directors, as opposed to the stockholders (and bondholders), exercises "real direction over the general policies of the corporation."[42] "Real direction," however, is not the same thing as responsibility and control. The directors may indeed also bear this (and almost universally do), but not by their function as elected representatives of the stockholders, to whom they are (at least nominally) responsible. This can be seen from Knight's idealization of the pure entrepreneur as "a man who borrowed all the resources for operating a business and then hired a manager and gave him an absolutely free hand."[43] Nevertheless, Knight considers it a myth to regard the large number of stockholders as the real owners.

The large number of stockholders in some of our great corporations is definitely misleading. Most of these do not regard themselves and are not regarded as owners of business. . . . The great companies are really owned and managed by small groups of men who generally know each other's personalities, motives, and policies. [44]

These "insiders," then, are the real entrepreneurs.

Knight further adds that "in general practice the ownership of property is necessary to the assumption of genuine responsibility."[45] He repeats later that "the basis of effective assumption of responsibility is necessarily either the ownership of property or the creation of a lien on future human productive power, and is in fact almost altogether the former."[46]

Knight makes no attempt to identify these insiders, whether by name, characteristics, or practice. His analysis is therefore less than complete on this matter. After all, however useful abstractions like the "pure entrepreneur" may be for economic theory, they must in the end be made to explain economic life as it is experienced.[47]

Perhaps more worrisome is the implication that there may be less than easy access to financial markets and as a result imperfect entry into the world of entrepreneurs. The laws of profit worked out on the basis of the perfect-entry assumption would certainly require substantial modification. This is particularly important today, in an era of transnational corporations, a small number of which account for the greater part of the gross national product in the United States. While it may be that most—though by no means all—people can turn entrepreneur, they can do so only in certain limited markets.

PROFITS AND ACCUMULATION

Knight's theory of profits certainly has little in common with the interest of the classical economists in the production of a surplus as an accumulation fund. But Knight does find an important connection between profits and accumulation. To be sure, "the first requisite of capital creation is the creation of a surplus, the production of more goods than are consumed . . . . This is the essential meaning of 'saving.' "[48] But the act of turning saving into new production must take place in an uncertain world. "Social progress on the material side is largely motivated by a desire to possess wealth." This is where profits enter, for "the role of uncertainty in connection with capitalization is to make it possible for an individual through superior judgment or good luck to obtain a large increase in his wealth in a short time."[49]

It is hardly novel to argue that profits serve as the engine of economic growth. What Knight brings to the argument, however, is the connection between uncertainty and the profits made in economic growth. With no uncertainty, there would be no profits. There might still be economic growth, says Knight, but apparently not as rapid. And that, for Knight, is the significance of private property.

Private property is a social institution; society has the unquestionable right to change or abolish it at will, and will maintain the institution only so long as property owners serve the social interest better than some other form of social agency.[50]

This he believes to be so, in the world of uncertainty; in a world of certainty it could not possibly do better.

In this way Knight returns in part to his earlier theme: "It is not too much to say that the very essence of free enterprise is the concentration of responsibility in its two aspects of making decisions and taking the consequences of decisions when put into effect."[51] Although ostensibly built on the foundations of the neoclassical equilibrium, Knight's theory of profits is really a long way from Walras. Indeed, it suggests that Walras's system failed to capture "the very essence of free enterprise." In this sense, Knight's work is a new benchmark not only in the theory of profits, but also in economic theory as a whole.

That Knight himself does not see it that way is perhaps understandable (his assertion that his work contains "little that is fundamentally new" is not false modesty); Marshall, after all, considered himself squarely in the classical tradition, even as his work supplanted that of Mill and Ricardo.[52] But more important, Knight's *approach* to economic questions *begins* from a genuinely neoclassical position; he accepts the theory of rent, interest, and wages put forward by his neoclassical forebears (even if he later "modifies" it by his own profit theory), and he looks to the market for explanations of fundamental economic phenomena.

But if his beginning is conventional, his end is nevertheless quite new and original. Knight discovers a role for the entrepreneur—or, better, for enterprise—in the market economy that had eluded neoclassical orthodoxy. The uncertainty theory makes clear that the problem lay precisely in that orthodoxy.

OTHER UNCERTAINTY THEORISTS

There have been several attempts to develop and extend Knight's uncertainty theory of profits. The more innovative and penetrating are those that do not confine themselves to Knight's restrictive neoclassical focus; they are examined in subsequent chapters. Here we mention those working essentially in the Knightian framework.

Burton S. Keirstead

Burton S. Keirstead attempts to further Knight's theory by analyzing expectations and decision-making under uncertainty. The most succinct summary of his theory is contained in G. L. S. Shackle's review of Keirstead's work, showing how "general expectations" and "particular expectations" are connected through policy decisions, horizon distance, and type of market to "windfall profits," "monopolist's profits," and "innovator's profits."[53] Keirstead's three types of profits differ from Knight's conception only at first sight; in reality, Keirstead attributes them all to dynamic phenomena that are subject to uncertainty.[54]

Monopolistic profits, formally distinguishable in a static model, may be altered over time, and their maximization over a period may call for a different policy from that which maximizes the instantaneous rate at which they are earned. Thus these surpluses may become the object of entrepreneurial planning for the future.[55]

Windfall profits are those arising from changes in the purchasing power of money.

General and particular expectations are simply those regarding the overall economic climate and those regarding the inputs and outputs of a particular firm, respectively. Though both types of expectations are made in an atmosphere of uncertainty, the degree of uncertainty is much less regarding general conditions—so much so, says Keirstead, that the business acts as if it were certain, and hence the term "subjective certainty."[56] In determining how decisions are made in an uncertain world, Keirstead follows Shackle in dividing the possibilities of future outcomes into favorable and unfavorable spectrums, each weighted with (subjective) estimated likelihood and each becoming telescoped into "focus gain" and "focus loss," respectively. The greater of these then determines the decision.

It seems evident that Keirstead's theory elaborates that of Knight without devising much of significance for profit theory. In fact, in explaining the origin of profits in the economy, Keirstead falls below the level attained by Knight.

J. Fred Weston

Weston wants not only to defend Knight against other profit theories but also to extend and develop this line of reasoning on profits. His analysis can be summarized in five points. First, he redefines risk and uncertainty. Uncertainty "involves future events about which there is incomplete knowledge or whose probability of occurrence is not 1." Risk is merely that uncertainty that is associated with an "undesirable event." Thus risk is now a subset of uncertainty.[57] This is aimed mainly at preventing the kind of mistake Weston feels has resulted from a misunderstanding of Knight's usage.

Second, the distinction of significance for profit theory is now between "transformable risk" and "nontransformable risk" (rather than between risk and uncertainty). The former involves not only "measurable risk" (the Knightian risk) but some unmeasurable risk as well, which may be reduced (or eliminated) through insurance, organized markets, laws, and so on. It is nontransformable risk that generates profit.

Third, profit is not the sole residual, or noncontractual, income; that is, some factors—for example, "ultimate decision-making," or entrepreneurship (which term, however, Weston shuns as misleading)—are not contracted for, and the net income over and above contractual factor payments includes returns to those factors as well as profit. The distinction between these latter and profit is that profit is not a return for any function—or, alternatively, a return for no function.

Fourth, as can be deduced from the above, profit must be the difference between *ex ante* and *ex post* incomes. That is, in a world of certainty there would still be a residual income, but this would simply compensate the "unhired" factors. It is the difference between this expected residual and the actual residual (i.e., the difference between expected compensation of unhired factors and the actual amount available to them) that constitutes profit.

Fifth, while it is true that the firm (or entrepreneur) tries to maximize this net residual, it is entirely wrong to say that the firm tries to maximize profits; this is, in the nature of things, impossible. Similarly, there can be no such thing as "normal" profit.

Two interesting conclusions follow. First, a competitive firm in short-run equilibrium in an industry in long-run disequilibrium—that is, the firm's marginal cost equals market price, and both are greater than average total cost—is not necessarily making profits. The difference between price and average cost is unit *quasi-rent*. It is only when expected costs (or expected price) differ from actual costs (or actual price) that profits or losses could arise.

Second, it is not necessarily true that a monopolist earns profit—indeed, it is probably not true. The differential return that he receives "is usually a differential wage, interest or rent return depending upon the means by which the monopolistic advantage was fashioned."[58]

For Weston, then, profit is not the residual income to a firm, but only the *unexpected* part of this residual; the rest goes to pay productive factors that are not operating under contract. Insofar as these uncontracted factors are simply land, labor, and capital, the residual includes implicit rent, wages, and interest, all distinguishable from profit; this is Knight's view. Weston, however, seems to have in mind some other factor (or factors) that is routinely not contracted for. It is never identified clearly, however, a serious drawback. Furthermore, the distribution of the residual, on whatever principle, provides the remuneration of this factor. This latter is therefore routinely subject to variable payment, not in accordance with productive services rendered; why and how this comes about is a matter in need of explication.

Weston concludes,

The "profit motive" is not the major source of economic incentives in a price economy. The payments anticipated by factors of all types motivate economic activity. This is to say that in a price economy, relative prices perform the function of providing incentives and of allocating resources.[59]

This follows from his analysis of profits. Weston's restriction of profits to a portion of the residual, the rest being income produced by noncontractual factors, necessarily restricts their significance. While his profits are generated, like Knight's, by differences in *ex ante* and *ex post* values in an uncertain world, they come in the end, unlike Knight's, to mean very much less.

Notes

1. Frank Knight, *Risk, Uncertainty, and Profit* (Chicago: University of Chicago Press, 1971), p. ix. Martin Bronfenbrenner refers to Knight's theory as "contemporary orthodoxy"; see his *Income Distribution Theory* (Chicago: Aldine Atherton, 1971), p. 366.

2. Knight, *Risk, Uncertainty, and Profit,* p. 19.

3. Ibid., p. 51.

4. Frank Knight, "Profit," in *Readings in the Theory of Income Distribution,* eds. William Fellner and Bernard F. Haley, pp. 539, 537, respectively; emphasis added.

5. Knight, *Risk, Uncertainty, and Profit,* p. 271.

6. Ibid., p. 51.

7. Ibid., p. 225.

8. Ibid., p. 213.

9. Ibid., p. 46.

10. Ibid., pp. 43–44.

11. Ibid., p. 213.

12. Ibid., p. 247.

13. Ibid.

14. William Fellner asserts that Knight fails to propound a theory of uncertainty, so that "in matters of uncertainty, to which frequency concepts are not applicable, 'anything goes.' " By contrast, Fellner wishes to fill this perceived void with subjective probability decision-making. But even this leaves him with little to say on profit origin: "About profits *ex post* —by which I here mean profits, *given* the amounts invested—one can only say that they depend on luck as well as the quality of the probability judgments by which the individual was guided." But in a world of uncertainty there are no standards by which to make good probability judgments. Fellner concentrates instead on *ex ante* profits—profits, that is, as a guide to economic decisions and activity—which is an entirely different matter. See William Fellner, *Probability and Profit* (Homewood, Ill.: Richard Irwin, 1965), pp. 30, 109.

15. Knight, *Risk, Uncertainty, and Profit,* p. 267.

16. Ibid., p. 268.

17. In a like vein, J. R. Hicks, following Joan Robinson, has come to criticize "steady-state" growth theory; see his "Some Questions of Time in Economics," in *Evolution, Welfare, and Time in Economics*, Essays in Honor of N. Georgescu-Roegen, ed. Anthony M. Tang et al. (Lexington, Mass.: D. C. Heath & Co., 1976).

18. Knight, *Risk, Uncertainty, and Profit*, p. 313.

19. Ibid., pp. 237–38.

20. Ibid., p. 268.

21. Ibid., p. 241.

22. Ibid., pp. 241–42.

23. Ibid., p. 271.

24. Ibid., p. 276.

25. Ibid., p. 227.

26. Ibid., p. 271.

27. Ibid., p. 280.

28. Ibid.

29. Ibid., p. 281.

30. Ibid., pp. 273–74.

31. Ibid., p. 317.

32. Ibid., p. 283.

33. Ibid., pp. 363–64.

34. See also below, p. 145.

35. Knight, "Profit," p. 537.

36. Knight, *Risk, Uncertainty, and Profit*, p. 227.

37. Ibid., p. 306.

38. Ibid., p. 278.

39. Ibid., pp. 294–95.

40. Ibid., p. 291.

41. Ibid., pp. 300–301.

42. Ibid., p. 291.

43. Ibid., p. 300.

44. Ibid., pp. 358–59.

45. Ibid., p. 309.

46. Ibid., p. 351.

47. This is in one sense the difficulty of the classical economists in reconciling the labor theory of value—their abstraction—with the cost-of-production theory, which is how pricing appears to take place.

48. Knight, *Risk, Uncertainty, and Profit*, p. 323.

49. Ibid., p. 333.

50. Ibid., pp. 359–60.

51. Ibid., p. 349.

52. Ibid., p. ix.

53. G. L. S. Shackle, "Professor Keirstead's Theory of Profit," *Economic Journal*, March 1954.

54. Burton S. Keirstead, *The Theory of Profits and Income Determination* (Oxford: Basil Blackwell, 1953), p. 15.

55. Ibid.

56. Burton S. Keirstead, *Capital, Interest, and Profits* (New York: John Wiley & Sons, 1959), p. 32.

57. J. Fred Weston, "A Generalized Uncertainty Theory of Profit," *American Economic Review*, March 1950, p. 43.

58. Ibid., p. 56. Anatol Murad suggests that it is senseless to identify the restriction of output with performing a function in any meaningful way; Weston replies that it may not be functional in terms of physical output, but in value terms it surely is—and this is all that matters for the economist. See "Comment" and "Rejoinder," *American Economic Review*, March 1951, pp. 164–69, 175–81.

59. Ibid., p. 60.

CHAPTER 7

The Incomplete Institutional View

The contract is the fundamental cornerstone of our country and baseball as well.

—*M. Donald Grant*
Chairman of the Board
New York Mets

Frank Knight clearly establishes a place for profits in neoclassical theory—not as a footnote or an appendix, but as the inevitable concomitant of uncertainty in the economy. In doing so, however, he also undermines two of the cornerstones on which that theory is based: general equilibrium and marginal productivity. With uncertainty—and its partner, time—factor incomes can correspond to *ex post* marginal products only by chance; the former are set by contract before the latter can be known. Profits and losses continually appear. No manner of economic adjustment can arrive at general equilibrium (again, except by chance), because at the end of any production or market period the future is still unknown; hence not only the amount but even the direction of the necessary "corrections" are unknown. If Knight then provides a theory of profits, he removes the cornerstone for neoclassical distribution theory in general.

Knight does reintroduce another avenue for economic inquiry, though he himself does not take it very far: the role of institutions.

Contracts and contractual incomes are clearly essential for him, and he does mention the problem of locating entrepreneurial activity in a world of corporations; nevertheless, Knight's comments on these matters are not firmly grounded in an overall theoretical base. By contrast, the work of Thorstein Veblen, John R. Commons, and to a degree John Hobson stresses institutions as determinants of economic activity, and therewith incomes. Although none offers a completely elaborated theory of profit origin, all contribute to an understanding of the context in which profit is possible.

CONTRACTS AND PROPERTY

The importance of contracts—and of private property, whose disposal implies the contractual relation—is underscored by Thorstein Veblen. He makes the often neglected point that property is a historical development.

The institution of ownership is ancient no doubt; but it is young compared with blood relationship, the state, or the immortal gods. . . . Freedom and inviolability of contract has not until recently been the unbroken rule. Indeed, it has not even yet been accepted without qualification and extended to all items owned.[1]

Veblen also outlines the subtle distinctions of property ownership at various phases of history. Originally, he argues, the right of ownership descended from the view that each individual has a natural right to use what he himself has created; that is, ownership meant ownership of one's own products. In contrast to this natural right of ownership is the ownership of, for example, natural resources. This latter

rests not on a natural right of workmanship, but on the ancient feudalistic ground . . . of seizure by force and collusion. The owners of these natural resources own them not by virtue of their having produced or earned them, nor on the workman-like ground that they are making use of these useful things in productive work. These owners own these things because they own them.[2]

Clearly, a system based on the production of profit cannot arise on the basis of the notion of property as solely the use of one's own products.

There prevails within the range of business traffic the presumption that there must in the natural course of things be a stable and orderly increase of the property invested. Under no economic system earlier than the advent of machine industry does profit on investment seem to have been accounted a normal or unquestionably legitimate source of gain. . . . This is reflected, e.g., in the tenacious protests against the taking or paying of interest and in the ingenious sophistries by which the payment of interest was defended or explained away.[3]

In contrast, "the normality, or matter-of-course character, of profits in the modern view is well shown by the position of those classical economists who are inclined to include 'ordinary profits' in the cost of production of goods.'"[4]

In presenting this historical perspective, Veblen is concerned to emphasize the underlying conditions under which profits arise (or could arise). Contained within is an implied critique of neoclassical, and classical, economic theory which views the separation of the factors of production from one another as "natural" or "normal" and takes this separation (if not necessarily the almost inevitably associated private ownership) as the foundation of economic theory for all economies.[5] He does not, however, go on to develop a theory of profits as such; nowhere does he seek to explain the origin of profits as a special category of income. More often than not, he treats all income arising from property ownership as a piece—and he includes profits therein.

Veblen does see distinctions between the various incomes. He certainly never believes either that profit is the same as a return on capital (in the financial sense) or that the rate of profit is, in equilibrium, zero. "In ordinary times . . . and under capable management, the current rate of business earnings exceeds the rate of interest by an appreciable amount."[6] On the whole, however, Veblen leaves off at observation, rather than constructing a real theory.

John R. Commons, a founder of institutional economics in the United States, built his system around property and contracts. He is at pains to reveal the true nature of this institution, how it has been overlooked by the classical and neoclassical economists and how much is therefore in need of reevaluation.

Like Veblen, Commons argues that the notion of property as "use-value"—that is, as the use of one's own objects—has changed with the changing economic order. The change is incorporated into, and indeed defined by, the legal framework within which man's activities take place; in fact, "the term 'property' cannot be defined except by defining all the activities which individuals and the community are at liberty or required to do or not to do, with reference to the object claimed as property."[7] This inverts the classical attitude toward economic ("natural") laws, as these were deemed immutable and not to be interfered with by ordinary legislation of men. For Commons, the rights and duties referred to are strictly man-made. Hence it is a delusion to attempt to formulate "natural economic laws" based on property considerations.

Indeed, this is the basic flaw in all of economics—it ignores the willful activity of people:

Economic theory, since the time of the Physiocrats, has endeavored to get rid of the human will and to explain economic phenomena, as we know them, in terms of physical and hedonic forces. . . .

But a volitional theory takes exactly the opposite point of view. Economic phenomena, as we know them, are the result of artificial selection and not of natural selection. Their evolution is like that of a steam engine or a breed of cattle, rather than like that of a continent, monkey or tiger. If you watch how the steam engine evolved from John Watt in 1776 to the Mogul locomotive in 1923 you will see how economic institutions evolved. . . . If you watch the development of the credit system out of the customs of businessmen in buying and selling, borrowing and lending, and out of the customs of courts in deciding disputes, according to the changing common rules, you will see how political economy evolved. . . .

The human will is always directing itself to investigation, explaining and controlling the limiting factors that obstruct its purposes at the moment and under the circumstances. It is always injecting an "artificial" element into the forces of nature.[8]

On the basis of such a "volitional theory" it might be expected that Commons would develop the importance of, for example, contracts in all economic phenomena—and in particular indicate the relation between profits and contracts. Like Veblen, however, he does not; he too inclines only toward observations and criticisms. For example,

The older theories of the classical economists, dominated by the idea of an automatic equilibrium which tends to bring fluctuating prices back to the normal costs, paid attention to the "cost of production." The modern institutional theories pay attention to the margin for profit which has no "normal" whatever.[9]

This follows a lengthy examination of a typical corporate income statement and the various accounting margins associated with revenue, cost, and profit. And while commenting on the institutional ambiguities inherent in various economic concepts—for example, the rate of profit—nowhere does Commons discuss the origin of profit itself; this is taken as datum. While he does indicate the fluctuating character of profits, he does not discuss the economic conditions that produce profit or loss in general.[10]

PROFITS, ENTREPRENEURS, AND CORPORATIONS

In the modern world of large corporations, it is not an easy task to identify the entrepreneur (as evidenced by the generally unsuccessful attempts of the nineteenth century and early twentieth century). Veblen explains why: he has disappeared. The captain of industry "is no longer the central and directive force in that business traffic that governs the material fortunes of mankind."[11] His real era extended from the Industrial Revolution to the beginning of corporation finance.

Veblen's "captain of industry" is the entrepreneur, or businessman, of the classical political economists who may indeed no longer be in existence.[12] But the duties of this classical entrepreneur are still being performed.

So the function of the entrepreneur, the captain of industry, gradually fell apart in a two-fold division of labor, between the manager and office work on the one side and the technician and industrial work on the other side. . . . The captain of industry developed into a captain of business.

Industry and business gradually split apart. . . . The employer-owners shifted farther over to their own ground as absentee owners, but continued to govern the volume of production and conditions of life for the working personnel on the businesslike principle of net gain in terms of price. [13]

But Veblen believes that this two-sided replacement has not been adequately identified by the economic profession. "In the manuals, the captain of industry still figures as the enterprising investor-technician of the days of the beginning, and as such he still is a certified article of economic doctrine under the caption of the 'Entrepreneur.' " [14] This, however, is not an accurate image of Frank Knight's position, whose pure entrepreneur is a very special character (even if no easier to find than the classical "captain of industry"). Nonetheless, it is likely that the general understanding of "entrepreneur" is not so different from Veblen's idealized conception—and caricature—of the "captain of business." He sometimes uses the word this way himself, charging that the *entrepreneur's* "furtherance of industry is at second remove, and chiefly of a negative character. In his capacity as *business* man, he does not go creatively into the work of perfecting mechanical processes and turning the means at hand to new or larger uses." [15] This latter is the work of engineers and technologists. The role of the entrepreneur, says Veblen, is only to *allow* the engineers to improve production, *or not*. Clearly, he is referring here to "captains of business." It should be remembered that Veblen also identifies these latter with his *absentee owners*, who under a different interpretation would be mere owners of capital and not "captains of business" or entrepreneurs in any sense at all. Veblen, however, suggests that they are not *that* far removed from business, not *that* "absent" from control—or rather, that there may indeed be a class of capital-owners (rentiers) whose *sole* economic "function" is to own (and hire out) capital; but there is no "pure" entrepreneur who owns nothing—those in ultimate control of business are also owners of that business. That is to say, these owners are "absent" only from the "industrial" (i.e., technological) side of business affairs.

In any case, this entrepreneur or captain of business cannot be earning profits for entrepreneurial activity in any usual sense (unless profits, too, are "chiefly of a negative character"). Commons echoes the spirit of Veblen's critique in remarking that "the public generally does not distinguish between getting rich by efficiency and getting rich by unloading dead horses on others. Each is equally honorable according to the customs of business and the *caveat emptors* of legality."[16]

Commons is more interested in the corporation as an entity than in entrepreneurs in any sense. He agrees with those who consider corporations profit-maximizers. "Individuals may have other motives, but when they enter corporations all other motives are eliminated. Corporations are institutions for profit, as churches are institutions for worship."[17] In analyzing the various accounting sheets for any particular corporation, however, he quickly comes to the conclusion that "it is evident . . . that there is no such thing as a 'normal profit.' "[18] This conclusion, reached by looking at the evidence, he feels is also correct theoretically—that is, there are no economic "laws" which produce a "normal" or uniform rate of profits. He continues by arguing for the necessity of examining corporations one by one in analyzing profits and profit origin: the conditions that produce profits for each firm are particular to the firm itself.

Thus does Commons zero in on exactly those features which are generally not analyzed, features which—like locational monopolies, brand names, advertising, and wage and salary differentials, among others—make one firm different from others. It is precisely these institutional, technical, and monopolistic (or oligopolistic) aspects which Commons feels are ignored by economic theory, with the result that economic theory cannot explain why a given firm earns a given rate of profits.

Unfortunately—though not surprisingly—Commons never takes these microeconomic building blocks and constructs a macroeconomic theory of profits. He does apparently believe that while profits may have no "normal" level, they are nevertheless a "normal" (i.e., regular) feature of the economy. That is presumably why he never bothers to explain their existence (origin) on a macro level.

Hobson, that early dissenter from Marshallian orthodoxy, has the most expansive view of the entrepreneur and thus sees the widest distribution of his income, profit. Entrepreneurial work is performed by financiers, corporate directors, salaried officials, stockholders, and inventors. The first group consists of "unspecialized 'capitalists,' promoters of companies, bankers, and other money-lenders, who deal in profitable notions, and whose productive function is to determine the application of real capital and labour to different industrial undertakings."[19] Financiers, that is, are by no means neutral in the process of capital investment; their decision-making in this regard is of the entrepreneurial sort. The same may be said of the ordinary stockholders, who "must be accredited some skill of discernment and judgment in choosing among the competing enterprises offered to him for investment."[20] The board of directors and the salaried officials of a corporation perform the work of general supervision, detailed management, and a portion of the financing of production. Inventors advance technology. All help make land, labor, and capital more productive than they would be were they employed by their owners. For this reason, profit

must include (a) the incomes of financiers so far as these exceed the normal interest upon the capital engaged in their profession; (b) the royalties and other payments made to inventors and patentees; (c) the fees of directors and the salaries of officials of companies, for though these can in some sort be set on a level with other labour markets, the work done for them belongs to the entrepreneur; (d) a portion of the so-called interest paid to shareholders who contribute ability in the selection of their investments.[21]

There are some problems here. Managerial salaries are contractual incomes, not residual payments. But Hobson views them as both more irregular and more speculative in character than the usual payments for labor; in this sense, the contract is but the form that disguises an at least partly noncontractual income. What part of the "interest" paid to stockholders constitutes profit is not clarified. Whether financier interest above the average rate may not be a monopoly income is not directly addressed by Hobson, neither is the question of whether a patent might not just as usefully be regarded as a quasi-rent. Indeed, in general, "it is necessary to admit that no practical theory of economic policy can be based on an attempt closely to discriminate between profit in the sense of 'rent of ability' and other payments which are inextricably mixed with it in the actual distribution of wealth."[22]

Despite the widespread nature of the profit payment, the number of entrepreneurs never grows so large as to compete away all profit.

The hypothesis that competition normally works as freely and as keenly among entrepreneurs as among labourers is notoriously false. It rests really upon an assumption that any worker is free to become a small employer, and any small employer to become a large employer. . . . If this assumption were correct, it is true that the gain of each progressive step in industry would pass to society as soon as it was open to the competing businesses in a trade. . . .

[But] the number of competing entrepreneurs buying the other factors, and seeing the product of their co-operative working, is much smaller than the number of separable units of labour-power, capital and land, which are competing to find purchasers, and the competition of the former is less keen, constant, and ubiquitous than that of the latter.[23]

Unfortunately, this seems to be more an observation than a theoretical necessity for Hobson. In any case, it does have an important implication: there is nothing in the economic system that distributes the gains of progress to the society at large, at least in any short period. Hobson goes even further: the profit reward may be "a far larger sum than is required to stimulate ability."[24]

In all this, it may be said that more questions are raised than answered. Who gets the profit reward? Where does it originate? Who is the entrepreneur? What does he do? All this remains clouded. But Veblen, Commons, and Hobson, in their neoclassical dissent, help to clarify the importance of institutional matters in unraveling the profit problem.

Notes

1. Thorstein Veblen, *Theory of Business Enterprise* (New York: Charles Scribner's Sons, 1904), p. 69.

2. Thorstein Veblen, *Absentee Ownership and Business Enterprise in Recent Times* (New York: B. W. Huebsch, 1923), p. 51.

3. Veblen, *Theory of Business Enterprise*, pp. 85–86.

4. Ibid., pp. 87–88.

5. Elsewhere the critique is explicit, as in his essays in Thorstein Veblen, *The Place of Science in Modern Civilization and Other Essays* (New York: B. W. Huebsch, 1919).

6. Veblen, *Theory of Business Enterprise*, p. 96.

7. John R. Commons, *Institutional Economics* (New York: Macmillan Co., 1934), p. 74.

8. John R. Commons, *The Legal Foundations of Capitalism* (New York: Macmillan Co., 1924), pp. 376–78.

9. Commons, *Institutional Economics*, p. 586.

10. Ibid.

11. Veblen, *Absentee Ownership*, p. 101.

12. John Kenneth Galbraith, recognizing the phenomenon, centers entrepreneurial power (of a diffused sort) in what he calls the "technostructure." See John Kenneth Galbraith, *The New Industrial State* (Boston: Houghton Mifflin Co., 1967), esp. chaps. 6 and 8.

13. Veblen, *Absentee Ownership*, p. 106.

14. Ibid., p. 107.

15. Veblen, *Theory of Business Enterprise*, p. 44; emphasis added.

16. Commons, *Institutional Economics*, pp. 584–85.

17. Ibid., p. 527.

18. Ibid., p. 570.

19. John A. Hobson, *The Industrial System* (London: Longman, Green & Co., 1910), p. 128.

20. Ibid.

21. Ibid., pp. 128–29.

22. Ibid., p. 134.

23. Ibid., p. 132.

24. Ibid., p. 131.

CHAPTER 8

Sraffa and the Surplus Revival

In matters of philosophy and science authority has ever been the great opponent of truth. A despotic calm is usually the triumph of error. In the republic of the sciences sedition and even anarchy are beneficial in the long run to the greatest happiness of the greatest number.

—*William Stanley Jevons*

The difficulties of the Walrasian equilibrium–marginal productivity combination in explaining the origin of profits—or explaining income distribution generally in a capitalist economy—are mirrored by Marshallian partial equilibrium analysis, especially the influential price theory. Piero Sraffa is foremost in arguing the logical inconsistency of Marshall's system as a foundation of neoclassical analysis, including value and distribution theory. Sraffa also begins a "return to the classics" by clearing up the hurdles Ricardo faced and then installing a price theory based on classical considerations. By focusing once again on production, Sraffa is able to restore the idea of a surplus whose allocation plays a crucial role in his price theory.

This restoration is not merely a revival by mimicry. Instead, Sraffa attempts solutions to two technical problems left dangling: finding an "invariable" measure of value and distinguishing between necessary and luxury goods.[1] There are also important implications for the theory of profit origin, although the formal constructive work in profit theory is left by Sraffa to be completed by others.

SRAFFA: RETURNS AND COMPETITION

Sraffa's first English critique of Marshall appears in his "The Laws of Returns Under Competitive Conditions."[2] His point is that perfect competition has a rather narrow application in the real world, and that the modifications required in the analysis to approximate real conditions are sizable, even in the cases of industries that have traditionally been considered competitive. His proof lies in an examination of the laws of increasing and diminishing returns and the supply curve. Sraffa states his intention not "to add anything to the pile" of the "qualifications, the restrictions and the exceptions" which "have eaten up, if not all, certainly the greater part of the theory," but rather simply to compile them and examine their combined impact.[3]

Sraffa discloses that the Marshallian supply curve, showing first increasing and then decreasing returns, is an attempted fusion of two separate classical considerations. Diminishing returns was long viewed as a consequence of the special conditions, in particular nonreproducibility, of natural resources, and was used to explain the rent of land; increasing returns "was much less prominent, as it was regarded merely as an important aspect of the division of labour." Thus, "in the original laws of returns the general idea of a functional connection between cost and quantity produced was not given a conspicuous place."[4] Such a connection is necessary, however, if the distribution of income is to be coherently presented as an outcome of the theory of value or price. Sraffa, therefore, in spotlighting the inconsistency of invoking supply and demand curves to determine price also provides a critique of neoclassical distribution theory.

With regard to diminishing returns, Sraffa sees two possibilities. If the fixed factor in the production of a particular good is a "considerable part" of the total quantity of that factor, then a small increase in production entails more intensive utilization of that factor, which "will affect in the same manner the cost of the commodity in question and the cost of other commodities into the production of which that factor enters."[5] And since the latter are usually substitutes of one degree or another, there will be a nonnegligible impact on the demand for the original good. This, however, violates the assumption of independence of supply and demand required for equilibrium under conditions of perfect competition. A similar result holds when considering cases where only a small part of the total of the constant factor is employed in the production of a good. Here,

a (small) increase in its production is generally met much more by drawing "marginal doses" of the constant factor from other industries than by intensifying its own utilization of it; thus the increase in cost will be practically negligible, and anyhow it will still operate in a like degree upon all the industries of the group.

And therefore, "the imposing structure of diminishing returns is available only for the study of that minute class of commodities in the production of which the whole of a factor of production is employed."[6] Unless factors are specified so narrowly that each industry may be said to be employing all of that factor (which would make meaningful economic analysis virtually impossible), diminishing returns has very little importance in actual markets.

Increasing returns fares no better with Sraffa, for when increasing returns is due to "those *external* economies which result from the general progress of industrial environment," they "must, of course, be ignored, as they are clearly incompatible with the conditions of the particular equilibrium of a commodity." Increasing returns due to a firm's internal economies, however, "must be put aside as being incompatible with competitive conditions." That leaves only economies which are internal to the industry but external to the firm—which, however, is "precisely the class which is most seldom to be met with."[7]

Sraffa argues, therefore, that to consider adequately decreasing and increasing costs it becomes necessary to turn away from the assumptions of perfect competition and examine instead the features of monopoly. This, he asserts, is even more definitely the case after reflecting on competitive industries in the real world. This is a somewhat paradoxical result, since it would appear that "when production is in the hands of a large number of concerns entirely independent of one another as regards control, the conclusions proper to competition may be applied, even if the market in which the goods are exchanged is not absolutely perfect."[8] This is not the case, however, and for two reasons. First, the assumption that the competing producers have no impact on the market price is invalid. Second, real producers generally operate under decreasing, not increasing, costs. That is, the output of a firm is determined not by the intersection of a perfectly elastic demand curve and an increasing marginal cost curve, but rather by a downward-sloping demand curve and diminishing (or constant) costs. Thus, it is not that the producer faces impediments through his own cost inelasticity, but rather the fact that a greater output, produced at either the same or lower cost, cannot be entirely sold without lowering the price—and thereby the profit position—or incurring prohibitively higher marketing costs.

This can happen, in a competitive industry, because consumers are *not* indifferent between the products of different firms. The various firms all have barriers which prevent, to one degree or another, other firms from entering their market. Whether for reasons of custom, confidence, location, personal acquaintance, or trademark, each firm has something of a monopoly over a segment of the market for a particular good.

THE MONOPOLISTIC DIGRESSION

Thus, one way of interpreting Sraffa's analysis is that the traditional assumptions of perfect competition must be discarded.[9] The existing analysis of pure monopoly is likewise unsatisfactory, however, though it was long ago recognized that the existence of monopoly introduces a very different element into the analysis, and that monopoly itself is a fount for a kind of profit. Adam Smith implies as much in his famous warning that businessmen always tend to collude when they meet, and also explicitly argues that monopolists make above average profits.[10] Neither Ricardo nor Mill departs from this view. A half century later, Cournot improves the formulation by showing that monopolists seek not the highest price but rather the highest profit, which entails both cost and elasticity of demand.[11] Marshall, in his own way, arrives at the same conclusion, that a monopolist adjusts his supply "in such a way as to afford him the greatest possible total net revenue."[12]

Monopoly, then, can be seen as a source of profits; profits—or at least above-average profits—are not competed away, since there is an absence of perfect competition. The monopolist's additional revenue represents a redistribution of income (away from all those who must pay the monopoly price), a *transfer* income rather than earnings for productive services in any functional sense. It is precisely this sort of income that vanishes in competitive equilibrium schemes, so that, again, insofar as profits arise from monopoly, general equilibrium is a no-profit position. The existence of profit, and therefore monopoly, would be a rebuff to equilibrium. But if profit arises only because of monopoly, and is therefore only a transfer income received due to a monopoly position, it is hard to quarrel with the view that profit results from exploitation.

Sraffa, however, does not wish to present real-world firms as pure monopolists, since the preponderance of cases falls short of such circumstances. The equilibrium position of firms is, in general, difficult to locate. He believes that although "the equilibrium is in general determinate [that] does not mean that generalizing statements can be made regarding the price corresponding to the equilibrium; it may be different in the case of each undertaking."[13]

This aspect of Sraffa's analysis and critique of neoclassical theory—in retrospect not the most fundamental—has some immediate echo. Indeed, his success in generating interest along these lines is indicated by Joan Robinson.

When I returned to Cambridge in 1929 and began teaching, Mr. Sraffa's lectures were penetrating our insularity. He was calmly committing the sacrilege of pointing out inconsistencies in Marshall (his article of 1926, also, was still reverberating). . . . The elders reacted by defending Marshall as best they could, but the younger generation were not convinced by them.[14]

And indeed Robinson applies herself to the problem, producing *The Economics of Imperfect Competition*.[15] She uncritically adopts

Marshall's "normal" profits, however, and therefore adds nothing to profit theory.

Simultaneously, in the United States, Edward Chamberlin, though not directly influenced by Sraffa, works out his theory of "monopolistic competition" along lines even more closely resembling the latter's suggestion.[16] His view is that economic reality is "a fusion of the hitherto separate theories of monopoly and competition."[17] This fusion he effects by treating each firm as a partial monopolist (or each monopolist as a partial competitor) because of product differentiation and obstacles to free entry. This produces "monopoly" prices: that is, the price is greater than average cost.[18] Where price equals average cost, "profits are just sufficient to cover the minimum necessary to attract capital and business ability into the field, which sum is always included in the cost curve."[19]

Chamberlin never defines profits explicitly, but it is clear that the firm, in his view, receives no residual income—after all costs, including capital cost, are paid—in a perfectly competitive situation. The most reasonable interpretation would appear to be simply that the only profits are "monopoly" profits—that is, profits appear only because there is no perfect competition.

At the same time, Chamberlin begins a critique of marginal productivity theory. He points out that it is impossible for all factors to be paid the value of their marginal products—except under the "unrealistic" assumptions of perfect competition—because the total product will be "over-exhausted." But he makes his peace by simply substituting the term "marginal revenue product" for the "value of the marginal product," without entering into a discussion of the deeper issues involved.

Robert Triffin takes monopolistic competition a bit further, at least as regards profit theory, accusing previous writers of "conventionalism" in their treatment of profits in this new, "imperfect" world.[20] For him the two main characteristics of profits are that they are "dynamic in their origin" and "institutional in their appropriation."[21] Furthermore,

the real relevance of change and uncertainty for a theory of profit is in the loosening of the actual link between productivity and remuneration. In a changing world, it cannot be said of profit, as of the elements of cost in the circular flow, that it just suffices to call forth precisely the "quantity of entrepreneurial services required." Such a quantity, theoretically determinable, does not exist.[22]

He ends with a modified Schumpeterian view.

The "surplus" [profit] soon melts away into increased remunerations to the various elements composing the firm. . . . The "profits" thus resolve themselves into rents in the Paretian sense, i.e., into increased remuneration of some factors (inelastically supplied), when one position of equilibrium is, in a dynamic world, replaced by a new one.[23]

Or, as he writes elsewhere, "profit, in the traditional sense of that term, dissipates itself among a number of different claimants."[24] Unfortunately, the upshot of all this is to put profits back on their previous feet—that is, still in need of an explanation. The world of less-than-perfect competition and monopoly may be the real world, but the world of zero profits is not. It is not until the work of Michal Kalecki that the connection between profit and imperfect competition is clearly drawn.[25]

SRAFFA: THE SURPLUS RESURRECTED

There is another path leading from Sraffa's little article which he only hints at there: "as a simple way of approaching the problem of competitive value, the old and now obsolete theory which makes it dependent on the cost of production alone appears to hold its ground as the best available."[26] It is Sraffa himself who follows up this hint, producing some thirty-five years later a theory of price that returns production to the center of analysis and identifies the cost of production as the analytical core of the theory. The starting point, in fact, is the technical circumstances of production: a given set of commodity outputs produced by another set of commodity inputs. If the system just reproduces itself, there will be one set of prices "which if adopted by the market restores the original distribution of the products and makes it possible for the process to be repeated."[27]

Alternatively, the system may produce a surplus over and above the commodities required for reproduction. The technical conditions are no longer sufficient to determine a consistent set of prices. In the no-surplus case, the "original distribution" is restored; with a surplus the distribution is not given, and indeed cannot be settled until prices are known. This follows from the need to have a uniform rate of profit on the means of production advanced, a heterogeneous set of goods which cannot be aggregated until their prices are known. "The result is that the distribution of the surplus must be determined through the same mechanism and at the same time as are the prices of commodities."[28]

That value and distribution are linked in this fashion is exactly the problem Ricardo faced and led him to "modify" his value theory, and is similar to the transformation problem in Marx.[29] Of course, the surplus could be distributed entirely to property-owners in the form of profits, leaving laborers only with a subsistence wage; in this case, prices would be determined entirely by production technique, and the problem of price changes would arise only with technical change. The possibility of wage-earners also sharing in the surplus makes the pricing problem more complex, for a change in the wage and profit shares will, in general, disturb prices.[30] As wages rise and profits fall, for example, goods that are more labor-intensive than average will have higher prices, as the higher wage is not offset by the lower rate of profit. Possibly there will be a good whose price is unaffected by such a change; this would require that the proportions of labor to means of production be the same as for the economy as a whole. Sraffa shows how an artificial composite commodity, dubbed the "standard" commodity, can always be constructed: it requires only that the various goods which make up this commodity have the same relative proportions as the goods required to produce it. This standard commodity then serves as an indicator of the effects of distribution changes on relative prices.

Armed with this construction, and the differences between this standard commodity (and the standard system based upon it) and the actual production processes, Sraffa is able to lay the basis for a profound criticism of neoclassical distribution theory. For one thing he notes the potential for "capital reversal."[31] A changing rate of profits has different effects on the value of two products (capital goods); in particular, it cannot be ruled out that as the profit rate steadily increases, first one capital good, then the other, then the first again, has a higher price. Not only is there no unambiguous relative valuation between the two goods, but their relative prices do not even exhibit a monotonic relationship with the rate of profit. "The reversals in the direction of the movement of relative prices, in the face of unchanged methods of production, cannot be reconciled with *any* notion of capital as a measurable quantity independent of distribution and prices."[32]

In like manner Sraffa discovers the existence of "reswitching." With two (or more) techniques for producing the same output, a shift in the wage-profit distribution of the surplus will affect, both through labor cost and the rate of profit "added on," the relative costs and prices, and therefore also the absolute profits for each technique. At some rates of profit, called "switch points," it is possible for different techniques to be equally profitable, but all possible rates of profit can be switch points only if the techniques are identical. Once again, it is impossible to identify a monotonic function that relates profit rates to the most profitable technique: a specific technique that is preferable to another at a given rate of profit may be less preferable at a higher rate but yet be preferable at a still higher rate. Thus reswitching of techniques occurs.

Taken together, these two discoveries play havoc with neoclassical attempts to tie profit to productivity. Indeed, Sraffa shows that it is impossible to identify any factor (capital) which can be used to *explain* profits, since the value of that factor already depends on *knowing* the rate of profit. Similarly, neoclassical attempts to posit factor substitution in production in accordance with the simple rule that as profits rise relative to wages labor will be substituted for capital cannot succeed. Thus, not only marginal productivity theory but also any "capital factor" theory is shown to be inadequate to explain the profit income.

At the same time, Sraffa's construction of the standard system and his analysis of the wage-profit share ramifications solve Ricardo's value problem and accomplish Marx's transformation of (labor) values into prices (of production). Regarding the latter, labor values are simply a special case of Sraffian pricing wherein the rate of profit is zero.[33] Thus Sraffa resurrects the classical notion of a surplus product as fundamental to the problem of distribution, returning production as well to center stage in the analysis.[34]

Much less is to be said regarding Sraffa's contribution to the perception of profit origin. He purposely leaves out an institutional setting for his analysis, so that his framework represents not so much an economy as such but rather an abstract analytical method which may just as well be used in examining a socialist economy as a capitalist one. In like manner, not only does Sraffa not address the issue of what exactly the wage-profit split is—that is, how it is determined—but he never discusses why there should be a profit income at all. It is technically feasible, in the Sraffian system, for labor to receive the entire surplus; how and why a situation could come about that non-laborers could receive part of this surplus remains unanswered.[35] Furthermore, the division of the nonlabor income is not taken up.

Still, Sraffa's system is more than simply a return to Ricardo. The surplus is admittedly a technical datum of an economy which has reached a certain level, but it is a result of the interconnected working of the entire economy; neither the surplus nor any part of it can be attributed to some subset of the inputs in the economy. And since Sraffa pointedly leaves out marginal changes in the data for his economy, no imputation is possible. Furthermore, he shows that the economic system itself cannot endogenously solve the wage-profit split issue, but that also implies that there are ambiguous limits to the wage share (up to the point where it is equal to the entire surplus) or the profit share (up to the point where it is equal to the entire surplus, if the subsistence element of the wage is considered separately), as implied by marginal productivity theory.[36] Last, Sraffa's profit includes what is otherwise a residual income, even if the absence of contracts or "natural" rates of return make this appear to be a moot point.[37]

Notes

1. Alessandro Roncaglia, "Sraffa and the Reconstruction of Political Economy," *Challenge*, January–February 1979, p. 51; reprinted in Alfred Eichner, ed., *A Guide to Post-Keynesian Economics* (White Plains, N.Y.: M. E. Sharpe, 1979), pp. 93–4.
2. *Economic Journal*, December 1926.
3. Piero Sraffa, "The Laws of Returns Under Competitive Conditions," *Economic Journal*, December 1926, p. 536.
4. Ibid., p. 537.
5. Ibid., p. 539.
6. Ibid.
7. Ibid., p. 540.
8. Ibid., p. 542.
9. Not that this saves the supply and demand analysis. See Alessandro Roncaglia, *Sraffa and the Theory of Prices* (New York: John Wiley & Sons, 1978), pp. 12–14.
10. See above, Chapter 2.
11. Smith could be interpreted as meaning the same thing without explicitly stating it. This can in no way diminish Cournot's contribution: even assuming Smith understood the point, he did not comprehend its importance.
12. Alfred Marshall, *Principles of Economics* (New York: Macmillian Co., 1948), p. 478.
13. Sraffa, "The Laws of Returns Under Competitive Conditions," p. 549.
14. Joan Robinson, *Collected Economic Papers*, vol. 1 (Oxford: Basil Blackwell, 1951), p. vii.
15. Joan Robinson, *The Economics of Imperfect Competition* (London: Macmillan & Co., 1959).
16. Allyn Young's influence in directing Chamberlin's interests toward these matters is well known and evident. See Young's "Increasing Returns and Economic Progress," *Economic Journal*, December 1928.
17. Edward Chamberlin, *The Theory of Monopolistic Competition* (Cambridge: Harvard University Press, 1958), p. ix. Chamberlin contrasts this view with Robinson's that monopoly could be said to be "swallowing up" competition.

18. Ibid., p. 111.

19. Ibid., pp. 21–22.

20. Robert Triffin, *Monopolistic Competition and General Equilibrium Theory* (Cambridge: Harvard University Press, 1962), p. 158.

21. Ibid. Later he again mentions—but does not discuss—institutions: "The distribution of profit among the entrepreneur and the owners varies in each case with the institutional setup governing their mutual relationships and under which production is taking place." Ibid., p. 179.

22. Ibid., p. 168.

23. Ibid., p. 173.

24. Ibid., p. 179.

25. See Chapter 10.

26. Sraffa, "Laws of Returns Under Competitive Conditions," p. 541.

27. Piero Sraffa, *Production of Commodities by Means of Commodities* (Cambridge: Cambridge University Press, 1960), pp. 3–5.

28. Ibid., p. 6.

29. See Jan Kregel, *The Reconstruction of Political Economy* (New York: John Wiley & Sons, 1973), pp. 23–24, for a view of how the technical similarity in the problems faced by Ricardo and Marx nevertheless refers to two different problems.

30. The only exception would be the unrealistic case in which all industries used the same proportions of labor to means of production.

31. Identified by Joan Robinson as the "Ruth Cohen curiosum"; see her *Accumulation of Capital* (London: Macmillan & Co., 1956), pp. 109ff.

32. Sraffa, *Production of Commodities by Means of Commodities*, p. 38.

33. See Jan Kregel, *Rate of Profit, Distribution, and Growth: Two Views* (Chicago and New York: Aldine Atherton, 1971), p. 20.

34. For a brief account of the significance of this concept, see Roncaglia, "Sraffa and the Reconstruction of Political Economy," pp. 49–50.

35. "Sraffa makes no attempt to explain how distribution is determined, and the use and creation of the invariable measure sought by Ricardo is compatible with any explanation of the distribution process" (Kregel, *Reconstruction of Political Economy*, p. 119).

36. Strictly speaking, marginal productivity theory asserts that higher wages are possible, but only at the expense of employment. See Roncaglia, "Sraffa and the Reconstruction of Political Economy," p. 53. Note that this also counters the old wage-fund doctrine.

37. In Sraffa's system it makes no difference whether the wage or the profit rate is determined first, leaving the other as the residual income.

CHAPTER 9

Profits and the Early Macro Theory

Nothing can be more childish than the dogma that because every sale is a purchase, and every purchase a sale, therefore the circulation of commodities necessarily implies an equilibrium of sales and purchases.

—*Karl Marx*

Even before the implications of the early criticisms of neoclassical distribution have time to sink in, Keynes launches an attack on other orthodox foundations. In particular, he focuses on the principle of effective demand, in the short period, for the economy as a whole.[1] This, it turns out, involves much more than merely generalizing from the knowledge of how individual economic units, whether households or businesses, act and interact.[2] Thus, macroeconomics is born. And the developing theory of economic aggregates carries with it some important insights into the process of income distribution. That the first macro theories do not successfully integrate these insights into a complete distribution theory is testimony both to the understandable priority given to the issue of effective demand and macroeconomic management, and to the complex, and at times paradoxical, character of macro-distribution theory.

KEYNES: THE WIDOW'S CRUSE

John Maynard Keynes himself is not primarily concerned with income distribution as such in any of his writings; nowhere does he set out to explain the origin or relative size of the various income classes. His work does take note of money wages and profits, though his "struggle of escape from habitual modes and expressions" on this score is hardly an outright success.[3] Nonetheless, his reconstruction of economic theory contains material of importance for profit theory.

It is in his *Treatise on Money* that Keynes first deals explicitly with profits, as elements in his "fundamental equations" on the value of money.[4] Here, Keynes seeks to explain how the price level is determined and how profits in particular affect prices. Income is defined to be the earnings of the factors of production—or, alternatively, the cost of production—and therefore consists of the sum of wages, rent and "regular monopoly gains," interest, and the "normal remuneration of entrepreneurs." The latter is a Marshallian relic: "The entrepreneurs being themselves amongst the factors of production, their normal remuneration . . . is included . . . in the costs of production."[5] Just what the entrepreneur contributes to production that suggests this classification is, however, not even whispered. Profits are something quite different, namely, the difference between actual sales proceeds and costs of production. Hence,

Whilst the amount of the entrepreneurs' normal remuneration must be reckoned, whether their actual remuneration exceeds it or falls short, as belonging to the income of the individuals who perform entrepreneur functions, the profits must be regarded, not as part of the earnings of the community (any more than an increment in the value of existing capital is part of current income), but as increasing (or, if negative, as diminishing) the value of accumulated wealth of the entrepreneurs. If an entrepreneur spends part of his profits on current consumption, then this is equivalent to negative saving.[6]

Keynes defines the "normal remuneration" of entrepreneurs as "that rate of remuneration which, if they were open to make new bargains with all the factors of production at the currently prevailing rates of earnings, would leave them under no motive either to increase or decrease their scale of operations."[7] Keynes is thus obviously echoing Marshall insofar as he treats entrepreneurs as having a "normal" remuneration, but neatly sidesteps the problem of whether this constitutes "profits," a return for a labor service, or pay for some other productive service (and if so, what kind). Nor does he close off the possibility that the normal rate is actually nil (though that is hardly to be expected).[8]

Keynes next defines savings as income minus expenditure on consumption. Since income has been defined *exclusive of profits,* savings are also *sans* profits. Therefore, "the value of the increment of wealth of the community is measured by Savings plus Profits."[9] Nevertheless, his earlier remark that consumption spending out of profits is "equivalent to negative saving" should apparently be taken to mean that actual saving *decreases,* because consumption expenditure out of profit income increases. Thus, while savings themselves do not include profits, what is done with profits can affect the level of savings.

Investment is then defined as the increase in the stock of capital. The value of investment is the value of the increment of capital (not the increment of the value of capital).

These definitions allow Keynes to write the overall price level as:

$$\pi = \frac{E}{O} + \frac{I - S}{O}$$

where π = price level, E = income, O = output, I = investment, and S = savings.[10] Since profits are the excess of the value of output over costs of productions, they can be written:

$$Q = (E - S + I) - E = I - S$$

where Q = profits. Hence profits are the difference between investment and savings. Therefore the equation for the price level may be written:

$$\pi = \frac{E}{O} + \frac{Q}{O}$$

This formulation yields a useful answer to the question of why profits, as defined, should arise at all. It might not be obvious at first glance why the value of output should deviate from its cost of production, but it is not difficult to see how investment could deviate from saving, in Keynes's definition. For example, consumers with an income of $150 million may decide to spend $100 million on consumption goods and save $50 million; but producers may have produced goods (whose total cost must be $150 million) in such a way that the consumption goods cost $90 million and investment goods $60 million. Then $100 million is actually spent on consumption, yielding a profit of $10 million, exactly the "excess" of investment over saving. It would appear, in fact, that profits (or losses) are likely to be the normal (i.e., the regularly occurring) case, and zero profits the fairly rare exception.

In this context Keynes's much-discussed remarks concerning the nature of profit appear:

There is one peculiarity of profits (or losses) which we may note in passing, because it is one of the reasons why it is necessary to segregate them from income proper. If entrepreneurs choose to spend a portion of their profits on consumption (and there is, of course, nothing to prevent them from doing this), the effect is to *increase* the profit on the sale of liquid consumption goods by an amount exactly equal to the amount of profits which has been thus expended. This follows from our definitions, because such expenditure constitutes a diminution of saving and thus an increase in the difference between I and S. Thus, however much of their profits entrepreneurs spend on consumption, the increment of wealth belonging to entrepreneurs remains the same as before. Thus profits, as a source of capital increment for entrepreneurs are a widow's cruse which remains undepleted however much of them may be devoted to riotous living. When, on the other hand, entrepreneurs are making losses, and seek to recoup these losses by curtailing their normal expenditure on consumption, i.e., by saving more, the cruse becomes a Danaid jar which can never be filled up; for the effect of this reduced expenditure is to inflict on the producers of consumption-goods a loss of equal amount.[11]

This is easily illustrated using the example already cited. Suppose the $10 million profit were not "invested," but spent instead on consumption. The total consumption expenditure of $110 million as against a cost of production of $90 million would now produce a $20 million profit total—of which $10 million is spent on consumption goods and $10 million is still available for investment (it is in this context that the suggestion to call profits "windfalls" might have some sense). It must also be pointed out that in the situation where entrepreneurs are incurring losses, an increase in consumption generally—which would decrease savings—would reduce or eliminate those losses.

Although Keynes remarks that this perhaps startling result—that profits are a "widow's cruse" and a "Danaid jar"—follow logically from his definitions, the result actually arises more as a consequence of the assumption of *fixed-output*. An increase in consumption spending is seen as causing the price of consumption goods to rise (in the same proportion) rather than speeding an increase in output. All the more surprising then that Keynes' theory of profits should be so closely paralleled later by Michal Kalecki, who treats what amounts to the opposite case; effectively, Keynes deals with vertical supply curves while Kalecki uses horizontal cost curves.[12]

This analysis of profits raises two related points. The first concerns the nature of profits. Profits appear in this system because of the limited fixed-output assumption or, rather, because the point-supply need not be—and probably is not—identical to the point-demand. The question then becomes whether or not this is more accurately treated as a quasi-rent. In a more elaborate framework, *uncertainty* is undoubtedly present (otherwise consumption expenditure need never deviate from cost of production), even though Keynes chooses not to stipulate it explicitly. Entrepreneurs are producing for an unknown demand at a future date, and their ability (whether through skill or luck) to meet future needs determines their profit margins. Thus the term "profits" would appear justified.

The second, related question is whether Keynes's point-demand and point-supply is not a step backward from the neoclassical demand and supply *functions*. This is no doubt true with regard to supply and demand considerations in and of themselves. But Keynes is more interested in something else, namely, time and uncertainty and their critical role in the economy—or, as he expresses it, decisions to produce and decisions to consume are made by different groups of people at different times, and there is no *a priori* reason that the two should coincide exactly. It is precisely this point that is significant for the later development of his "general" theory.

Keynes does find his way back to equilibrium theory, however. The existence of profits (or losses) leads to price instability. This results not only from the existence of a profit term in the price equation, but also from the fact that entrepreneurs would bid up (or down) the remuneration to factors, thus affecting the first term in the price equation as well. There is an equilibrium solution in this system, however, and the condition for it is not difficult to meet—not in theory, at any rate. The banking system is capable of altering the rate of interest, affecting thereby both investment and saving, and therefore of compelling an equality between the two. Keynes concludes,

It is important for the reader to appreciate that the definition of Profits given above, and the division of the total value of the product between what we call Income or Earnings and what we call Profits, are not arbitrary. The essential characteristic of the entity which we call Profits is that its having a zero value is the usual condition in the actual economic world of today for the equilibrium of the purchasing power of money.[13]

That profits are forced to zero in equilibrium should not obscure the very different character of Keynes's analysis from the Marshallian or Walrasian version. For Keynes, entrepreneurs are implicitly different, as is the *mechanism* for equilibrium—namely, the price level. Thus it is not because profits are zero that equilibrium is reached, but rather because equilibrium is reached that profits are zero.

KEYNES: THE GENERAL THEORY

By the time Keynes comes to write the *General Theory,* he has altered his outlook fundamentally.[14] He finds the definitions contained in the *Treatise on Money* no longer suited to his purpose.

In my *Treatise on Money* I defined income in a special sense. The peculiarity in my former definition related to that part of aggregate income which accrues to the entrepreneurs, since I took neither the profit (whether gross or net) actually realized from their current operations nor the profit which they expected when they decided to undertake their current operations, but in some sense (not, as I now think, sufficiently defined if we allow for the possibility of changes in the scale of output) a normal or equilibrium profit; with the result that on this definition saving exceeded investment by the amount of the excess of normal profit over the actual profit. I am afraid that this use of terms has caused considerable confusion. . . . For this reason, and also because I no longer require my former terms to express my ideas accurately, I have decided to discard them.[15]

In Keynes's new schema, "the entrepreneur's income . . . is taken as being equal to the quantity, depending on his scale of production, which he endeavors to maximize, i.e., to his gross profit in the ordinary sense of the term."[16] That is, gross profit is equal to the gross revenue minus factor cost minus "user cost."[17] The entrepreneur's net income, or net profit, is equal to gross profit less supplementary cost, the latter being "the depreciation of the equipment, which is involuntary but not unexpected."[18] The gross profit concept is meant to be used when the entrepreneur's decisions regarding production are at issue, while net profit is reserved as the proper concept in affecting consumption decisions.

Thus Keynes abandons the zero-profit equilibrium theory (he also abandons the "widow's cruse"—but for a different reason, namely, the possibility of changes in output).

In this context arises the question of the exact level profits can be generally expected to attain, and why. In the passage quoted above, Keynes refers to normal or equilibrium profits, to which he returns.

The long-period cost of the output is equal to the expected sum of the prime cost and the supplementary cost; and, furthermore, in order to yield a normal profit, the long-period supply price must exceed the long-period cost thus calculated by an amount determined by the current rate of interest on loans of comparable term and risk, reckoned as a percentage of the cost of the equipment.

Or, in case the rate of interest is figured as a "pure" (i.e., riskless) rate, "the long-period supply price is equal to the sum of the prime cost, the supplementary cost, the risk cost and the interest cost.''[19] The apparent implication is that the "normal" rate of profit equals the pure rate of interest, though why that should be so fails to engage Keynes in the *General Theory*. The key problem— the explanation of the origin of profits, "normal" or otherwise— remains undiscussed.

Keynes thus discovers, by his nonsolution, the magnitude of the profit problem. He recognizes its importance, albeit indirectly, in his theory of equilibrium of the *Treatise*, on the one hand, and in his theory of production of the *General Theory*, on the other. More important, he brings to the study of profits those key issues to economic theory in general, namely, uncertainty, time, and the macro system. The full integration of profit theory into these concepts remains an abandoned waif.

BOULDING'S PROFIT RECONSTRUCTION

Kenneth Boulding constructs—or, as he sees it, reconstructs— both a micro- and a macroeconomic model of the economy. The latter is in some sense built on the former; yet as Keynes showed, in the world of macroeconomics things are often not a microeconomic blowup. This is perhaps nowhere more true than in the theory of (aggregate) distribution. Boulding notes that "the distribution of national income between labor and non-labor income, is not determined directly by the wage bargain or by the productive efficiency of management, but by a combination of other factors" which, at first sight, seem to have little if anything to do with distribution.[20]

Boulding's analytical technique is to treat all economic units— namely, businesses and households—from a balance-sheet point of view. From the fundamental identity that assets must equal liabilities, by aggregating over all businesses he reaches the macroeconomic identity that the net worth of all businesses is equal to the sum of their stock of money, the value of their stock of real goods, and the net debt of households to businesses. Thus:

$$G_b \equiv M_b + Q_b + (K_h - K_{h'})$$

Differentiation with respect to time yields

$$dG_b \equiv dM_b + dQ_b + (dK_h - dK_{h'})$$

The change in the net worth of businesses is simply business savings. Boulding regards this latter identity as significant in that it shows business savings as being determined by factors other than direct decisions to save, so long as these other factors are decided independently. Furthermore, total profits of business are equal to business savings plus business distributions—namely, interest and dividends—which Boulding writes as:

$$V \equiv dG_b + D$$

Hence, he concludes, "business decisions to save, as reflected in dividend policy, determine not business savings but the level of profits itself," achieving Keynes's "widow's cruse" theorem for an economy with variable output.[21]

Boulding tries to make this result—which he expects the reader to have difficulty grasping—more understandable through a small illustration.

Suppose for instance, that business savings, as given by the various items . . . which determine the net increase in business assets, i.e., in business net worth, are 10 billion. If businesses expect a profit of 30 billion and decide to save 12 billion they will distribute only 18 billion; hence actual profits will turn out to be 28 billion instead of 30, and in spite of the decision to save 12 billion businesses will succeed in saving only 10 billion.[22]

This example serves to underline the assumptions needed for the conclusion. First, businesses are acting according to the *expectation* of profits, not realized profits (a point not sufficiently emphasized by Boulding). Second, businesses' decisions regarding the size of distributions (i.e., dividends) are also made with regard to expected, not realized, profits.[23] Third, neither businesses' decisions to save nor businesses' decisions about the size of distributions have any effect on the realized net increase in assets—that is, on the level of business savings. The difficulty in evaluating the accuracy or usefulness of this last assumption is that Boulding does not explain how the true determinants of profits—namely, dM_b, dQ_b, and $(dK_h - dK_h)$ in the foregoing equation—operate to increase net worth.

In one sense they have no effect at all. If, for example, a firm sells some of its inventories, its cash account, M_b, would increase, but its stock of goods, Q_b, would decrease correspondingly. All transactions on the balance sheet are of this compensating character. Boulding has something more complex in mind; in his preface he criticized modern economists for, among other things,

a general failure to distinguish between two very different processes in economic life, the exchange or payments process on the one hand, by which existing assets, including money, are circulated among various owners, and the processes of production, consumption, income and outgo on the other, by which assets are created, destroyed, and accumulated.[24]

The latter processes, however, need elaboration in this context. Boulding himself decides later that the amount of business distributions "is likely to be correlated with profits: the higher profits, the higher will distributions be," thus inverting causation to the orthodox sequence.[25]

The total product, net of depreciation, equals household consumption plus the increase in the stocks of goods of both households and businesses (the money supply being assumed constant), or in Boulding's notation:

$$P_n \equiv C_h + dQ_h + dQ_b$$

From before:

$$V \equiv dG_b + D$$

$$dG_b \equiv dM_b + dQ_b + (dK_h - dK_{h'})$$

Substituting,

$$V \equiv dM_b + dQ_b + (dK_h - dK_{h'}) + D$$

Or

$$V \equiv dQ_b + T$$

where T, the "transfer item," is defined by the above identities,

$$T \equiv dM_b + (dK_h - dK_{h'}) + D$$

Since the total product is divided between profits and wages, it follows that wages equal the consumption of households plus the increase in the stock of goods of households (together called "household absorption") minus the transfer item. That is,

$$W + V \equiv P_n \equiv C_h + dQ_h + dQ_b$$

And therefore,

$$W \equiv C_h + dQ_h + dQ_b - (dQ_b + T)$$
$$\equiv C_h + dQ_h - T$$

From these results he derives the conclusion that

> The *distribution* of the product between wages and gross profits is determined by two elements: the *composition* of the product absorption on the one hand as between business investment and household absorption, and a transfer factor which we add to business absorption to get the total of profits, and subtract from the total of household absorption to get wages.[26]

This he illustrates with the diagram in Figure 1, and thus an increase in T will increase profits at the expense of wages.

Hence the seeming paradox that "extending credit to households has a directly favorable effect on gross profits, and shifts the basic distribution pattern from labor to non-labor income."[27] This kind of credit has the effect of increasing household indebtedness to business, thereby increasing the transfer factor. This, in turn, is supposed to increase profits. Yet it is possible to question the conclusion, for the whole point of consumer credit is to enable the consumer to purchase stocks of goods held by businesses. Thus an

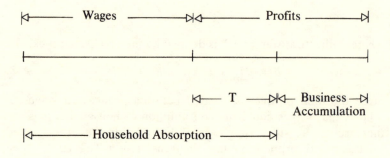

Figure 1. Boulding's Profits

increase in consumer credit will decrease one element of profit (viz., dQ_b) exactly as much as it increases another (viz., T) leaving the total profit unchanged. No other interpretation appears to make sense, especially since Boulding identifies consumer credit with installment credit and customer charge accounts.

A similar result holds with respect to business debt to households. Boulding reaches the conclusion, which again he considers paradoxical, that "the greater the volume of securities sold to households, the more the distribution pattern is shifted toward wages and away from gross profits."[28] But again, the problem is that, for example, if the public buys the securities with cash, businesses' stock of money increases proportionately to the increase in their indebtedness to households, thereby exactly offsetting the wage bill effect.

Regarding the last factor in the transfer item, Boulding comments:

We know far too little, however, about the determinants and effects of business distributions. In so far as business distributions consist of contractual interest payments, there is no great problem, for in any one period these can be taken as approximately given, though there is a real long-run problem, regarding the historical determinants of the volume of contractual debt. The short-run problem, however, is mainly that of the determinants of dividend distributions on shares.[29]

This, however, is unpredictable, as there is wide room for subjective motives to have effect. But the general impact he has already analyzed.

In any case, the transfer item as a whole is only one determinant of the level of profits, and the smaller one; the larger determinant is the level of business accumulation. This is directly subject to business control and constitutes a fairly unambiguous element in the profit term.

Concerning what might in this context be called net profits, namely, gross profits minus interest and rent, Boulding makes only one point.

> The distribution of non-labor income between contractual income (interest and rent) and residual income (profits) at any one time is historically determined by the nature and extent of contractual obligations, and does not present many serious theoretical problems.[30]

This can be deemed unduly optimistic, especially in light of his own analysis of interest.

> If, therefore, there was a reasonably competitive market in all securities, the concept of a long-run rate of interest would make a good deal of sense, and it would bear a close relationship to the long-run rate of return on "real assets," i.e., the rate of profit. Two things, however, weaken the usefulness of such a long-run concept. One is the very rapid fluctuations in the rate of profit itself and, still more, in the expected rate of profit on new asset combinations. . . . A more fundamental weakness, however, arises from the imperfection of the securities market.[31]

Serious theoretical problems are posed unless one is ready to interpret this to mean that the true determinants of interest are not necessarily of theoretical interest to the economist.

KALDOR: KEYNESIAN PROFITS

Nicholas Kaldor, in his essay "Alternative Theories of Distribution," makes an explicit and somewhat more successful attempt to extend the work of Keynes to the theory of distribution; he himself refers to his work as a Keynesian theory.

Keynes, as far as I know, was never interested in the problem of distribution as such. One may nevertheless christen a particular theory of distribution as "Keynesian" if it can be shown to be an application of the specifically Keynesian apparatus of thought and if evidence can be adduced that at some stage in the development of his ideas, Keynes came near to formulating such a theory.[32]

Kaldor begins by assuming full employment (a rather perverse "Keynesian" assumption that is dropped later on). Income is divided into "Wages and Profits (W and P), where the wage-category comprises not only manual labor but salaries as well, and Profits the income of property owners generally, and not only of entrepreneurs."[33] Investment is inscribed as equal to savings, and savings are made from both profits and wages. Therefore

$$I = s_p P + s_w W = s_p P + s_w (Y - P) = (s_p - s_w)P + s_w Y$$

and

$$\frac{P}{Y} = \frac{1}{s_p - s_w} \cdot \frac{I}{Y} - \frac{s_w}{s_p - s_w}$$

where s_p, s_w are the savings propensities out of profits and wages, respectively, I is investment, and Y is total income. This approach has validity only if $s_p \neq s_w$; and, in particular, Kaldor shows that $s_p > s_w$ is required for stability.[34] Reality appears to fit this assumption. "Thus, given the wage-earners' and the capitalists' propensities to save, the share of profits in income depends simply on the ratio of investment to output." More specifically, the "interpretative value" of this model relies on the "Keynesian hypothesis that investment, or rather the ratio of investment to output, can be treated as an independent variable, invariant with respect to changes in the two savings propensities s_p and s_w."[35]

If workers consume their entire income (i.e., if their propensity to save is zero), the above relation simplifies to:

$$P = \frac{1}{s_p} \cdot I$$

This indicates that profits exceed investment by the amount of capitalists' consumption: Kaldor has here extracted a symbolic statement of Keynes's widow's cruse conclusion or Kalecki's "capitalists earn what they spend" result.[36] He also points out that it is the exact opposite of Ricardian and Marxian distribution theory in that the latter determine profits as a residual, whereas here profits are determined first, leaving wages as the residual.

Kaldor notes four limitations on the above model. (1) Wages must be sufficient to sustain the labor force; therefore profits cannot be so great as to leave too little for subsistence wages. (2) The ratio of profit to total output must not fall below a minimum determined by risk, necessary to induce capitalists to invest. (3) The same ratio must not fall below a minimum determined essentially by the degree of monopoly. (4) The capital-output ratio must be independent of the rate of profit; otherwise the investment-output ratio, which is related to the capital-output ratio, will be dependent on the rate of profit and the model will be circular, not determinate. If the first of the above conditions is not met, "we are back at the Ricardian (or Marxian) model."[37] Furthermore, there will be unemployment. This also occurs if the second or third conditions are not met. One wonders whether Kaldor considers unemployment possible only under these conditions.[38]

Kaldor's theory is, in an important sense, a precursor of the modern macro-distribution theories. Kaldor deals, as they do, with an economy of just capitalists and workers and seeks to explain the incomes of these two classes—profits and wages—as the fundamental distributive problem.[39] Kaldor views, as some others do, the determination of profits as prior to that of wages. And, as shown above, his theory yields the widow's cruse/Kalecki paradox under the same simplifying assumptions. Further, the connection between profit, investment, and growth is drawn in a novel way that will become one of the hallmarks of the newer theory. Perversely, and less commendably, Kaldor assumes a given output, associated with full employment (except in the cases cited, where his theory breaks down), in order to render his model determinate. An alternate approach is to retain output as a variable; the additional factor necessary to determine profits is the relative share of output going to profits and wages, essentially given by the degree of monopoly.

Hence the priority of the relative determination of income over the actual size of the two incomes. Kaldor believes this must be either wrong or tautological, depending on the particular presentation.[40] Nevertheless, this alternative version has the advantage of incorporating a variable output level, surely a more "Keynesian" image than the fixed-output model that belongs to the pre-*General Theory* era. In this respect, Kaldor does not provide a generalization of Keynes, but rather a special case. It is the Kalecki version of macroeconomic theory suggested in the above alternative which provides the basis for further analysis of profit.

Still, Kaldor's claim to have provided a theory of distribution for the Keynesian framework is intriguing and not a false scent, for as he remarks, "I am not sure where 'marginal productivity' comes in, in all this."[41] It does not come in at all: not because Kaldor has replaced it, but rather because he has made it redundant by constructing a model on assumptions that avoid the issue.

Notes

1. "When Keynes was writing *The General Theory,* his main difference from the school from which he was struggling to escape lay in the recognition of the problem of effective demand, which they ignored. It was for this reason that he put everyone from Ricardo to Pigou into one category, and for this reason that he overvalued Malthus." Joan Robinson in Alfred Eichner, ed., *A Guide to Post-Keynesian Economics* (White Plains, N.Y.: M. E. Sharpe, 1979), p. xi.

2. This is now enshrined in textbooks as the fallacy of composition.

3. The words are from John Maynard Keynes, *General Theory of Employment, Interest, and Money* (New York: Harcourt, Brace & World, 1964), p. viii.

4. John Maynard Keynes, *A Treatise on Money* (London: Macmillan & Co., 1965).

5. Ibid., pp. 123–24.

6. Ibid., p. 124.

7. Ibid., pp. 124–25.

8. Keynes notes that some have suggested the use of the term "windfalls" rather than "profits" to label this somewhat unorthodox category of nonincome, but he finds that even more misleading. G. L. S. Shackle argues that Keynes is really only making a distinction between *ex ante* and *ex post* here: income is expected, therefore *ex ante,* income; sales proceeds, equal to income plus profits, is actual, therefore *ex post,* income. See G. L. S. Shackle, *Keynesian Kaleidics* (Edinburgh: Edinburgh University Press, 1974), pp. 17–21.

9. Keynes, *Treatise on Money,* p. 126.

10. This equation derives from the fact that the price level is the value of all goods divided by output; $E - S$ is the value of consumption expenditure, I is the value of investment. This requires, however, a correct choice of units. Keynes *defines* his unit so that "a unit of each good has the same cost of production at the base date " (ibid., p. 135). Also, the implication is that profits are not spent on consumption goods (or, for Shackle, consumption expenditure is taken *ex ante*); profits are dealt with separately.

11. Ibid., p. 139.

12. See Chapter 10.

13. Keynes, *Treatise on Money*, p. 156.

14. See also Keynes's remarks in the "The Great Slump of 1930," in *Collected Writings of John Maynard Keynes*, vol. 9, *Essays in Persuasion* (London: Macmillan & Co., 1972), esp. pp. 130–34.

15. Keynes, *General Theory*, pp. 60–61.

16. Ibid., pp. 53–54.

17. User cost, U, is given by: $U = (G' - B') - (G - A_1)$ where $A_1 =$ value of finished output purchases from other entrepreneurs, $G =$ value of capital equipment at the end of the production period, $B' =$ optimal sum spent on maintenance and improvement of capital if it had not been in use, and $G' =$ value of capital at the end of the production period if it had not been used, but B' had been spent on it.

18. Ibid., p. 56.

19. Ibid., p. 68.

20. Kenneth Boulding, *A Reconstruction of Economics* (New York: John Wiley & Sons, 1950), p. 174.

21. Ibid., p. 249.

22. Ibid., p. 250.

23. This has been criticized as unrealistic. See J. Johnston, "A Note on Professor Boulding's Macro-Economic Theory of Distribution," *Economic Journal*, March 1952, pp. 190–91.

24. Boulding, *Reconstruction of Economics*, p. ix.

25. Ibid., p. 261.

26. Ibid., p. 252.

27. Ibid., p. 255.

28. Ibid.

29. Ibid., p. 256.

30. Ibid., p. 246.

31. Ibid., p. 282.

32. Nicholas Kaldor, *Essays in Value and Distribution* (Glencoe, Ill.: Free Press, 1960), p. 227.

33. Ibid., p. 229.

34. This at first sight odd-looking condition is explained simply by the fact that if capitalists and workers act alike, one more element of indeterminateness is introduced.

35. Ibid., p. 229.

36. On Kalecki, see Chapter 10.

37. Ibid., p. 234.

38. This is one aspect of Weintraub's remark that Kaldor ignores supply phenomena. See Sidney Weintraub, *An Approach to the Theory of Income Distribution* (Philadelphia: Chilton Co., 1958), pp. 105–6.

39. James Tobin finds this insufficiently general, dealing only with two "factors" rather than with any (arbitrary) number. Kaldor replies, quite accurately, that macroeconomics is more than just a random aggregation of microeconomic terms. See James Tobin, "Towards a *General* Kaldorian Theory of Distribution," and Nicholas Kaldor, "A Rejoinder to Mr. Atsumi and Professor Tobin," both in *Review of Economic Studies*, February 1960.

40. This is in reference to Kalecki; see Kaldor, *Essays in Value and Distribution*, pp. 224–26.

41. Ibid., p. 236.

CHAPTER 10

Post Keynesian Profit Theory

It cannot be denied that there is something scandalous in the spectacle of so many people refining the analysis of economic states which they give no reason to suppose will ever, or have ever, come about.

—*Frank A. Hahn*

The emergence of macroeconomic theory provides a new setting for distribution theory. Although Keynes's concentration on effective demand phenomena and short period analysis tends to obscure the significance of the new perspective for profit theory, his emphasis on imperfect expectations in a world of uncertainty, occurring in real time, is more than just suggestive. "It is from this point that Post Keynesian theory takes off. The recognition of uncertainty undermines the traditional concept of equilibrium."[1] But other elements are necessary as well, derived in large part from Michal Kalecki.

The Post Keynesian profit construction replaces the marginal productivity-general equilibrium twins that proved so fruitless in understanding the profit income with savings ratios, degree of monopoly, investment decisions, and the classical surplus. The main conclusions seem to be: "Investment largely governs profits, and profits largely comprise the savings magnitude. The low savings propensities of wage earners, and the high savings ratios associated with profit incomes, enter in a crucial way in determining employment, income, and income growth."[2] In this context, profits refer to property income in general. The distillation of a special profit income distinct from the other nonwage income is likewise accomplished, by explicitly incorporating the social and institutional basis of economic activity into economic theory.

KALECKI: MONOPOLY AND SURPLUS

Michal Kalecki may be best known for his independent discovery of the main elements of "Keynesian" economic theory, but his writings, much more than those of Keynes, deal directly with the theory of income distribution in general, and the theory of profits in particular.[3] His contributions in this area have a significant influence on the development of modern economic theory.[4] Kalecki finds it impossible to incorporate his insights into output and distribution into the old value/price framework, however, and therefore elaborates a new scheme. This alternative to Marshallian and Walrasian analysis, running along lines suggested by Sraffa, becomes one foundation for modern versions of the classical surplus theory as well as for the new Cambridge (England) economic theory.

Kalecki considers that as far as price determination is concerned, goods must be divided into two separate categories. The first is "demand-determined" and consists mainly of raw materials and primary agricultural products. Here supply is inelastic over the short run and "an increase in demand causes a diminution of stocks and a consequent increase in price." The second is "cost-determined" and consists generally of "finished goods." For these, supply "is elastic as a result of existing reserves of productive capacity. When demand increases it is met mainly by an increase in the volume of production while prices tend to remain stable."[5] Kalecki is primarily interested in the latter category.

Clearly, the existence of "reserves" and increasing production with no increase in price is incompatible with perfect competition and increasing marginal costs. Kalecki believes that increasing marginal costs characterize only those goods whose prices are demand-determined, and not, therefore, industrial goods. In industry, constant (or even decreasing) costs prevail, at least over the relevant range; imperfect competition prevents production from being pushed up to the marginal-cost-equals-price equilibrium.[6] Indeed, Kalecki is quite close to Sraffa's conclusion that "the supply schedule with variable costs cannot claim to be a general conception applicable to normal industries [wherein] the cost of production . . . must be regarded as constant in respect of small variations in the quantity produced."[7] In a slightly altered context, Kalecki defends his assumption of excess capacity:

In the real world an enterprise is seldom employed beyond the "practical capacity," a fact which is therefore a demonstration of general market imperfection and widespread monopolies or oligopolies. Our price formula though quite realistic is not applicable in the case of free competition.[8]

In pricing its output, a firm uses a markup formula based on its own average prime costs—wages and materials—and the prices of other firms.[9] Specifically, $p = mu + n\bar{p}$, where p = price of the firm's output, u = firm's prime cost, and $\bar{p}$ = weighted average of other firm's prices. "The coefficients m and n characterizing the price-fixing policy of the firm reflect what may be called the degree of monopoly of the firm's position."[10] An increase of $\frac{m}{1-n}$ indicates a higher degree of monopoly.[11] Ordinarily this occurs through (a) increasing "concentration in industry leading to the formation of giant corporations," (b) "sales promotion through advertising, selling agents, etc.," (c) increasing overhead cost relative to prime cost, and (d) the strength of trade unions.[12] Clearly, increasing concentration and increasing sales through successful promotion increase a firm's markup and represent, in that sense, an increase in the degree of monopoly. The latter two may be gratuitous; strong trade unions, for example, may not affect the firm's markup but only initiate a wage-price spiral. In any case, the first two suffice to explain most changes. Note that technology does not directly affect the degree of monopoly (though it clearly affects price, through unit prime costs); the degree of monopoly must be considered a subjective element.

Kalecki then proceeds to determine the distribution of national income; in particular, he seeks to establish the relative share of wages. If the ratio of total proceeds to prime cost in an industry is denoted by k, then overhead cost plus profit can be written as $(k - 1)(W + M)$, where W, M represent total wages and total material costs, respectively. Therefore,

$$ w = \frac{W}{W + (k - 1)(W + M)} = \frac{1}{1 + (k - 1)(1 + \frac{W}{M})} $$

gives the wage share in the value-added in the industry. The value of k is clearly determined by the degree of monopoly—except in those industries whose products are "demand-determined" (agriculture and mining), as also real estate, finance, trade, communications, and public utilities. Since the relative share of wages in the value-added these latter sectors is negligible, Kalecki writes that "broadly speaking, the degree of monopoly, the ratio of prices of raw materials to unit wage costs and industrial composition are the determinants of the relative share of wages in the gross income of the private sector."[13] Industrial composition enters the relation because k, $\frac{W}{M}$ may both be different for various industries within the "cost-determined" group and because the relative importance of the sectors not in this group play a determining role. Kalecki also notes that the degree of monopoly tends to rise over time, while both the industrial composition and the materials-to-wage-cost ratio show no long-run tendency.

The gross national product, in a closed economy with neither government spending nor taxation, will be equal to the sum of gross profits and wages and salaries, on the one hand, and gross investment and consumption on the other hand. "The income of capitalists or gross profits includes depreciation and undistributed profits, dividends and withdrawals from unincorporated business, rent and interest."[14] Thus, Kalecki is here considering only two classes—workers and capitalists—with two basic income classes. If the further simplification that workers consume their entire income is made, it follows that gross profits are equal to gross investment plus capitalists' consumption.[15]

Since capitalists' decisions can affect investment and consumption, but not profits (not directly, that is), the former must determine the latter; in Kaldor's phrase, "capitalists earn what they spend and spend what they earn."[16] This at first sight paradoxical result is easily explained. An increase in consumption by one capitalist creates profits for those firms whose goods it buys, plus wages for workers in those industries. The wages in turn are spent on wage-goods, creating profits and wages again. In the limit of this process the total increase in profits will exactly equal the increased capitalist spending. This result holds only for capitalists collectively and not for any one individually.

Total wages in this system are determined by profits and the "distribution factors"—i.e., degree of monopoly, materials-to-wage-cost ratio, and industrial composition. Once decisions are made regarding the size of investment and capitalists' consumption, and given the distribution factors, both profits and wages in these sectors are determinate.[17] Profits in the wage-goods sector must equal the sum of wages in the first two sectors (since the wages in these sectors must be spent on wage-goods while the profits in the wage-goods sector must be spent in the other sectors). Again the distribution factors determine the size of wages in this third sector, and therefore the size of the sector as a whole, which is exactly equal to total wages.

From the earlier result that gross profits must be equal to gross investment plus capitalists' consumption, a further result is obtained by subtracting capitalists' consumption from both sides: gross savings equals gross investment. This relation holds independently of the rate of interest.

In the present conception investment, once carried out, automatically provides the savings necessary to finance it. Indeed, in our simplified model, profits in a given period are the direct outcome of the capitalists' consumption and investment in that period. If investment increases by a certain amount, savings out of profits are *pro tanto* higher.[18]

It is true that Kalecki does not describe in detail the financial side of this process which goes to guarantee his "real" result. His conclusion seems even more contradictory as a result. After all, where do the capitalists get the money to spend on consumption and investment? Surely not from credit, as this implies the prior existence of profit. From each other? That seems to be what he is saying, yet conflicts with common sense.

The answer to some opaqueness in grasping Kalecki's reversal of the usual direction of causation between profits and investment (and capitalists' consumption) lies in Marx's "realization of profits" concept. For profit to be realized, output must be sold, and at a price greater than wage cost. Clearly, the consumption demand of workers equal to total wages cannot be sufficient for profits to emerge; the latter requires a demand surpassing that of workers alone, namely, capitalists' consumption and investment—which is Kalecki's point and is tied in with his notion of the degree of monopoly, in need of greater elaboration.[19]

Kalecki's use of a gross profits concept to include all property income follows Marx's surplus value abstraction. On occasion he goes beyond this simplification and considers distinctions between entrepreneurs and rentiers; this remains, however, of distinctly secondary importance.[20] This can be justified for many purposes, employment theory in particular.[21] It leaves more work to be done on profit theory, however.

ROBINSON: PROFITS AND CAPITALISM

Joan Robinson is known for sifting over a wide range of important issues in economic theory, including prominently her work on income distribution. An unrelenting critic of neoclassical theory, Robinson simultaneously develops her own theory out of her critical perspective and furthers her criticism based on her constructive work.[22]

Robinson begins by insisting that the problem of profit is a theoretical riddle for the capitalist economy. To be sure, other economic systems contain analogous features, but profit is not one of them.

In an economy where manufacture is carried on by artisans, the earnings of labor, capital, and enterprise cannot be distinguished as separate sources of income. . . . When employment for wages becomes the main form of production, the division [of labor] is horizontal, between income from work and income from property. Profit as a distinct category of income is a characteristic of industrial capitalism. [23]

In like manner, a cooperative society must make decisions regarding present and future consumption, the latter secured at the expense of the former (or present leisure). Here,

neither the cost nor the proceeds are homogeneous and both contain psychological elements; the relation between them can be represented as a rate of return only by adopting some more or less arbitrary convention of measurement. However, the general idea of a present sacrifice yielding future advantages is clear enough. What has it got to do with the rate of profit on capital? In such a community, the current output of consumption goods, and the future benefit of higher consumption or more leisure, will be distributed among its members on some principle or other; the means of production belong to the community as a whole and the distinction between income from work and income from property has no meaning for them. [24]

Thus, income distribution is a process occurring under definite social and economic conditions and institutions, not a "natural" process that cuts across diverse societies and ages. [25] Specifically, "in a capitalist society, property is owned by a small number of individuals who hire the labor of a large number at agreed wage rates . . . and the excess of the product over the wages bill then appears as income from property." [26] Here, the classical surplus reappears. That it should seem to be an income attributable to property is due entirely to the character of the economic institutions.

Besides wage-earners, the economy has entrepreneurs, rentiers, and landlords. An entrepreneur is one who can command sufficient finance to set about employing labor. Rentiers are owners of financial property of any kind; thus, stockholders, bondholders, and banks all fit into this category. Land differs from capital in both technical (land is not generally augmentable) and social (landowners form a distinct social and political class) characteristics; therefore landlords are considered separately. In any case, these three categories are not exclusive regarding individuals; in particular, it is to be expected that an entrepreneur is also a rentier.

The familiar problem of locating the entrepreneur in the modern corporation is handled by focusing on the function, not the person.

The "entrepreneur" in modern conditions is a very amorphous conception; all the same, decisions concerning the conduct of a business must get themselves taken, whether by individuals or by interaction between individuals, and it is perhaps, legitimate to think (with due reservations) of a decision taking entity, embodying the policy of a firm, and by an anthropomorphic turn of speech, to refer to "him" as an entrepreneur.[27]

Stockholders in general are not entrepreneurs, but rather outside lenders of a peculiar sort. There is a smaller group of insiders, however, who have "large and permanent holdings in a particular business and take an active interest in its affairs" and fulfill at least some of the functions of the entrepreneur.[28] How to identify these insiders in a particular case is left open, as is the question of who performs the rest of the entrepreneurial functions. It is not crucial in this context, however, for there is no corresponding income.

Here, wages, rent, and interest are clear enough: "wages (including salaries) represent contractual payments for work of all kinds, rent is a contractual payment for the hire of land and buildings, and interest is a contractual payment for the loan . . . of finance." (That contracts are involved underscores her recognition of uncertainty, and entrepreneurial expectations not being fulfilled.) On the other hand,

profit is not such a simple concept. We shall use the expression *quasi-rent* to mean the excess of proceeds over running-costs of a business; and *profit* to mean the excess of quasi-rent over rent and the amortization required to maintain the capital of the business.[29]

Interest and dividends are paid out of profits, while the remainder is returned to the firm, leaving no special entrepreneurial income. Instead, the entrepreneurs' income "is made up of salaries (in the case of hired managers) and of personal allocations of profits, interest and dividends which they receive in their capacity as rentiers."[30] This entrepreneur should not be confused with the neoclassical one who invariably *expects* entrepreneurial income, however often he is disappointed in the general equilibrium state.

The classes of income correspond roughly with these social classes, but that is no justification for assuming a connection between incomes and productive services. In particular, profit exists because "under the prevailing rules of the game, anyone who can command finance can employ factors of production in such a way as to produce a selling value of product that exceeds the wages and rent bill involved in employing them."[31] Why this is so needs further explanation.

On the assumption of no saving out of wages, the wage bill in the consumption goods sector equals the sales of consumption goods to those workers. However,

workers engaged on investment [goods] and rentiers . . . are also buying commodities. This makes it possible for the selling value of commodities to exceed their wage cost. Looking at the same thing in another way, if the sales value of commodities were no greater than their wages cost, no one except the workers engaged in producing them could consume anything at all. [32]

That is, the existence of quasi-rent is equivalent to the condition that workers are engaged in producing investment goods and/or rentiers exist who must consume some of their rentier income. Furthermore, "each entrepreneur is better off the more investment his colleagues are carrying out. The more the entrepreneurs and rentiers (taken as a whole) spend on investment and consumption, the more they get as quasi-rent."[33] Here is the "capitalists earn what they spend" conclusion of Kalecki.

One other condition must also be met. "For profit to be obtainable there must be a surplus of output per worker over the consumption per worker's family necessary to keep the labor force in being."[34] That is, the techniques of production must be sufficient to produce more than workers' consumption.[35] While Robinson does not dwell on this point, her earlier remarks may be taken as indicating the significance of the existence of a surplus, while at the same time emphasizing the importance of the different institutional arrangements that effect its distribution.

The existence of a technical surplus is not a sufficient condition for profits to be realized. It is also necessary that entrepreneurs should be carrying out investment. The proposition that the rate of profit is equal to the ratio of accumulation to the stock of capital (when no profit is consumed) cuts both ways.

And thus "there are two opposite kinds of stagnation to which capitalist economies may be subject—stagnation due to technical poverty and stagnation due to satiety."[36]

Profit, then, is a part of the quasi-rent that is initially returned to the firm under the direction of an entrepreneur. Both depreciation and rent must then be paid out of quasi-rent. Apparently, rent could never become so large as to eat up profits. For this to occur, diminishing returns would have to have gotten completely out of hand, a condition surmountable by investment in land. Interest, which is paid out of profits, can similarly never eliminate dividends and retained earnings ("pure" profits). Only under "ideal conditions of perfect tranquility [would] the rates of interest . . . be equal to the rate of profit." Such tranquility never in fact exists— uncertainty is always present—and profits therefore exceed interest. "The level of interest rates is therefore not closely tethered to the level of profits and enjoys . . . a life of its own."[37]

One further clarification must be made. For the entrepreneur to make investment decisions, he must compare not *amounts* of profit but *rates* of profit. This turns out to be a considerable puzzle, not least because the ratio of profit to capital is a hopelessly "foggy notion," for "to express profits as a rate we must know the value of capital." Since the value of capital depends on being able to discount a stream of expected earnings by the rate of profit itself, this is not possible. "In reality, to find the expected rate of profit which governs investment decisions is like the famous difficulty of looking in a dark room for a black cat that probably is not there."[38] Working with the notion of the realized rate of profits has its own intricacies in that, whatever meaning it might have, it cannot generally be used to make investment decisions. That could make sense only if the economy "is growing smoothly in the conditions of a golden age, with expectations being continuously fulfilled and therefore renewed."[39] This is precisely the case where interest would absorb all profits, since the absence of uncertainty removes any reason for the rentier to accept anything less. And reality is never a tranquil golden age anyway; hence "the rate of profit on capital is neither uniform throughout an economy nor steady through time."[40] Thus, "to give a true account of realized returns is like the famous difficulty of the chameleon on a plaid rug."[41]

Nonetheless, Robinson still considers that "the concept of the normal rate of profit determined by investment and the propensities to save provides the framework of a general theory within which detailed analysis can be built up."[42] This has legitimacy in a macroeconomic context only if the existence of profit has already been explained and the determinants of "normality" have been uncovered; illegitimate is a postulate of normal profits. Hence her conclusion that her theory "provides Marshall with the basis of a theory of the rate of profit and the rate of interest, but it does not provide what he was looking for—a justification of the rentier income."[43]

WEINTRAUB: UNCERTAINTY AND AGGREGATE SUPPLY

Sidney Weintraub's distribution synthesis begins with the aggregate supply function. Aggregate proceeds for a given level of employment (and therefore of output, given the structure and technology of production) are equal to total wage costs, fixed payments (including rent and interest), plus a residual:

$$Z = wN + F + R$$

The residual, R, is a "catch-all category termed profits," though obviously it can be decomposed into depreciation allowances, indirect taxes, variable interest charges, etc., as well as profits proper."[44] Furthermore, "fixed payments are correctly conceived as rigid only for temporary and minor output variations; otherwise they are more variable than a tight interpretation would suggest."[45] Nevertheless, this approach presents the outlines of a profit theory, as suggested by the diagram in Figure 2, where, given an employment level N_1, total proceeds are given by N_1C, total wages by

N_1A, and fixed costs by AB ($= F$). Hence gross profits, R, are equal to BC. As employment (and output) increases, so will profits.

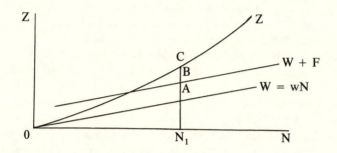

Figure 2. Weintraub's Profits

Weintraub defends this profit concept, criticizing both the "normal" profit scheme and the "pure" profit scheme, arguing that the latter "becomes in a way the most barren pill of all, for such income vanishes after the factor flux so that its magnitude is always pressing toward zero as resource adaptations are executed."[46] Instead, the network of contract agreements entered into by the entrepreneur who requires productive services—which produce wage, rent, and interest payments—freeze production costs at current expectations, allowing profits, under conditions of change and uncertainty, to emerge. "Profits . . . represent the unexpected surpluses ascribable to unforeseen demand-cost changes which, in degree, contradict the premises on which the agreements have been based."[47] Alternatively,

zero profits would entail that all firms, lenders, and resource owners generally, correctly perceive the employment level and the Z-W-gap. [see Figure 2] . . . Merely to state the problem in this way is to acknowledge the inevitability of the profit residual."[48]

Thus, profits result from an uncertain future dealt with by the institution of the contract. To cope effectively with this uncertainty, business turns to agreements for compensation over time, rendering this aspect of cost fixed (that is, certain, barring only default).

Without such contracts, borrowing would be impossible, and the use of productive equipment would require their ownership. Contracts are also valuable to business for reasons of liquidity. In addition,

speculative valuations attached to an asset by virtue of long-run forecasts may also render purchase agreements prohibitive; loft space in centrally located urban slum areas provides a case in point: differences in capital valuations may thus impede ownership transfer while rental agreements become a feasible and equitable solution.

In sum, "diversity of forecasts and risk aversion thus account for contractual modes of hire."[49]

It is the rigidity of payments in a contractual economy that allows profits to emerge. Or, again, when "contracts appear in the economy, a profit trail is almost inevitable."[50]

The profits-as-unexpected-surpluses notion suggests a windfall character to profits. Weintraub also notes that the difference between contractual payments, agreed upon *ex ante*, and the *ex post* imputed values of productive factors might be viewed as a kind of exploitation by the entrepreneur. This would require that losses be treated as exploitation of the entrepreneur by resource-owners. Furthermore, the implied judgment that factor owners "deserve" the full imputed value of the services of their resources is at odds with the very logic of the analysis, for the economic rationale for such a distribution scheme requires a world of certainty.

Likewise, a theory of profits as a series of windfall gains to the entrepreneur is not very promising. Here, the prices arrived at in the contract are treated as those that would produce the no-profit equilibrium position if the future turns out to be exactly like that of the "best guess" in some appropriate sense, of the participants (or perhaps the prediction of the "best" econometric model). This is clearly a contradiction; equilibrium requires *knowledge*, not guesses. In addition, the ever-present nature of profits (and losses) would imply continuously produced windfalls, surely a pointless terminological confusion.

Weintraub, too, tries to locate the entrepreneur in the modern economy, acknowledging that "he has proved a very elusive figure to track down."[51] Like Robinson, he identifies no one individual, but all of those who undertake the various aspects of entrepreneurial activity. Specifically excluded is the ordinary stockholder. Assigning to the latter the entrepreneurial function is

like charging each individual citizen with the ultimate conduct of foreign policy; because of the imperfections of democracy in general, and the democracy of corporate control in particular, this attempt to personify the entrepreneur seems insecure.[52]

Rather, it is all those who are in some degree or another responsible for corporate policy who are the entrepreneurs.

But—and this is crucial—not all of those who function, at least partially, as entrepreneurs recoup profits. "The entrepreneurial function is directed and executed with an eye toward profit-making; *the sharing of profits is an entirely different matter.* Entrepreneurial actions result in profits; profit-sharing presents some transfer aspects."[53] This, just as much as Knight's uncertainty, cuts the umbilical cord binding "contribution" to production with receipt of income.

This, however, does not result in misallocation of resources, since "it is a caricature of economic analysis to insist that profits are the key to resource use: with full certainty, with prices and costs known, profits are simply nonexistent, so that rents comprise the residual-income category to be maximized."[54] Therefore the view of profits as resource-allocator is mistaken anyway.[55] And with uncertainty, "current profits . . . provide at best only evidence of past structural distortion and scant hint to the future."[56] In an uncertain world, there is, and can be, no infallible guide to maximally efficient resource allocation.

Weintraub also works out his profit theory on the basis of the Kalecki-inspired insights, explicitly introducing the overall price level. Thus, as before,

$$Z = PQ = wN + F + R$$

where P is the price level and Q is the real output. Therefore,

$$P = w\left(\frac{N}{Q}\right) + \frac{F}{Q} + \frac{R}{Q} = \frac{w}{A} + \frac{F}{Q} + \frac{R}{Q} = k \cdot \frac{w}{A} = \frac{w}{A\theta}$$

where $A = \frac{Q}{N}$ is the average product of labor, k is the markup over unit labor costs, and $\theta = \frac{1}{k}$ is the wage share. There would be no meaning attached to this equation unless k had some (relative) stability. Weintraub argues this to be the case: whether for structural-institutional reasons, or competitive-monopolistic ones, k has remained roughly constant in terms of the gross business product in the United States.[57] As a result, "the price level is a consequence of money wage and productivity forces."[58]

The following identities may then be introduced:

$$C \equiv P_c\, Q_c \equiv W_c + U_c$$

$$I \equiv P_i\, Q_i \equiv W_i + U_i$$

$$Z \equiv C + I \equiv W + U \equiv (W_c + W_i) + (U_c + U_i)$$

where $$U = F + R.$$

In this formation all nonwage income is temporarily aggregated. C and I refer to consumption and investment, respectively, and the subscripts indicate activity in the particular sectors.

From the Keynesian identity of investment and savings, and from the "all and nothing hypothesis"—workers spend all their income, capitalists spend none of their income—the following result:

$$I = S = U$$

$$C = W = W_c + W_i$$

$$U_c = W_i$$

Given any I-value U is determined. Then, a pricing mechanism in the investment goods sector—i.e., a wage-cost markup of the type already indicated—gives the wage share in this sector, and therefore nonwage income in the sector as well. A pricing mechanism in the consumption goods sector then suffices to determine all magnitudes.

Subsequent modification brings in the "largely and something" hypothesis that wage-earners spend most, but not all, of their income, and nonwage-earners spend some but not much, of theirs. The main inferences remain.[59] In addition, the effects of monopoly, money, and wages can be easily analyzed, as can the significance of the distribution of U into its F and R components. A rise in monopoly power, leading to a price increase, will increase the nonwage income share and decrease employment. Tight money in this situation would only curtail investment, thus further increasing unemployment, without affecting prices. On the other hand, should an increase in money wages generate a proportionate price increase, it will "shift the income from rentiers to profit recipients, thereby lightening the debt burden. Further, the stock market need not be free of money illusion; higher money profits can affect equity prices disproportionately," thus influencing real investment.[60] Weintraub clearly demonstrates the usefulness of the new profit theory.[61]

POST KEYNESIAN MACROPROFITS

Probably the most important aspect of these macro theories is their radical departure from marginal productivity as a theory of income distribution. This is accomplished—in varying degrees by the individual authors—by focusing on financial as well as real matters (including consideration of the *money* wage and treating interest as a return to financial capital), by incorporating at least some aspects of monopoly and by recognizing the importance of uncertainty and the contractual network brought into being to deal with it. Tne result is that the profit residual is given a new life.

There are three income classes here—income from labor services, income from ownership (whether of capital or land), and profits.

For productivity imputations there are really only two productive agents, personal labor services and the services of instruments, whether land or equipment. Distributive payments, however, emanate out of the contractual arrangements between entrepreneurs who organize resource use and resource owners. At a minimum three income payment categories must be recognized: for personal services, for the use of money or things, and a residual of "gross" profits accruing to the firm for which the contractual decisions for the other services are made. Without this classification marginal productivity theory is bereft of a theory of profits so that, in describing income division under capitalism, it has effectively eliminated the unique profit component which distinguishes capitalistic institutions for resource organization from socialist counterparts.[62]

While profits are thus *ex post* residuals, the Kalecki conclusion seems to suggest the opposite, namely, that investment produces an *a priori* determination of profits. This is not necessarily the case, however. In Weintraub's scheme, for example, the unit wage is exogenous; the pricing mechanism determines the share of wages, and investment and profits therefore decide total wages.

Kalecki relies on the fact that perfect competition is nonexistent and proceeds to develop a theory for "semi-monopolistic" conditions. This includes markup pricing reflecting the "degree of monopoly" which largely governs profits, indeed, produces profits. This should not, however, be confused with the earlier identification of profits with "imperfections" in the market, since Kalecki considers "perfection" not only unrelated to the real-world economy, but also both misleading and false. The early Keynes suggests that profits over and above "normal" remuneration of entrepreneurs arise because of the separation—in time, place, and person—between investment and savings decisions, producing a difference between cost of production and overall sales value. Both Robinson and Weintraub present larger frameworks within which to view the entire distributive process. Both incorporate uncertainty and institutional elements, with the latter including not only contracts and corporations but also the organization of finance. It is these elements that are crucial in the reconstruction of profit theory.

Notes

1. Joan Robinson, "Foreward," in Alfred Eichner, ed., *A Guide to Post-Keynesian Economics* (White Plains, N.Y.: M. E. Sharpe, 1979), p. xi.

2. Sidney Weintraub, *Keynes and the Monetarists* (New Brunswick, N.J.: Rutgers University Press, 1973), p. 140.

3. See, inter alia, George Feiwel, *The Intellectual Capital of Michal Kalecki* (Knoxville: University of Tennessee Press, 1975) and Joan Robinson, *Collected Economic Papers* (Oxford: Basil Blackwell, 1965, 1973), vol. 3: "Kalecki and Keynes"; vol. 4: "Michal Kalecki." Oskar Lange writes, however, that Kalecki's model "is often wrongly reckoned with those based on Keynes' theory; in fact it is derived from the Marxist theory of reproduction and accumulation." Oskar Lange, *Political Economy*, trans. A. H. Walker, vol. 1 (London and New York: Pergamon Press, 1974), p. 309.

4. At least with regards to the various critical schools, even if mainstream neoclassical thinking tries to remain untouched. See esp. Weintraub, *Keynes and the Monetarists*, "Marginal Productivity and Macrodistribution Theory."

5. Michal Kalecki, *Selected Essays on the Dynamics of the Capitalist Economy, 1933–1970* (Cambridge: Cambridge University Press, 1971), p. 43.

6. He cites the work of Sraffa, Robinson, and Chamberlin in this regard. See Michal Kalecki, *Studies in the Theory of Business Cycles, 1933–1939* (New York: Augustus M. Kelley, 1966), pp. 50–52.

7. Piero Sraffa, "The Laws of Returns Under Competitive Conditions," *Economic Journal*, December 1926, pp. 510–11.

8. In *Readings in the Theory of Income Distribution*, W. Fellner and Bernard F. Haley, eds. (Philadelphia: Blakiston Co., 1946), pp. 204–5.

9. Kalecki's later formulation is given here in lieu of his earlier one.

10. Kalecki, *Selected Essays*, p. 45.

11. Proof: The original equation can be written as

$$\frac{p}{u} - n\frac{\bar{p}}{u} = m$$

This must hold up even in the case where $\bar{p} = p$, hence

$$\frac{p}{u} - n \frac{p}{u} = m, \quad or \quad \frac{p}{u} = \frac{m}{1-n}$$

Obviously, an increase in $m/(1-n)$ reflects a higher markup.

12. Ibid., pp. 49–50.
13. Ibid., p. 64.
14. Ibid., p. 78.
15. Kalecki's allowance for workers' saving and government activity in an open economy can be found in ibid., pp. 82, 84–86. Cf. Peter Erdos and Ferenc Molnar, "Profit and Paper Profit: Some Kalecki Evolution," *Journal of Post Keynesian Economics*, Fall, 1980.
16. Nicholas Kaldor, *Essays in Value and Distribution* (Glencoe, Ill.: Free Press, 1960), p. 230.
17. Kalecki is viewing the economy as a three-sector system, with investment-goods, wage-goods, and capitalists' consumption-goods as the three sectors.
18. Kalecki, *Selected Essays*, p. 83.
19. On this, and on the question of changes in the degree of monopoly, see Paul Davidson, *Theories of Aggregate Income Distribution* (New Brunswick, N.J.: Rutgers University Press, 1960), pp. 53–54.
20. Kalecki, *Studies in the Theory of Business Cycles*, p. 43, and Michal Kalecki, *Essays in the Theory of Economic Fluctuations* (New York: Russell & Russell, 1972), p. 87.
21. Kalecki shows that given the degree of monopoly, any increase in any of the subcategories of gross profits will have the same impact in increasing the national income and therefore employment (*Selected Essays*, pp. 94–95).
22. For a brief statement of the development of her thinking on these issues, see the two introductions to Joan Robinson's *Economic Heresies* (New York: Basic Books, 1971), as well as her "Marginal Productivity," in *Collected Economic Papers*, vol. 4.
23. Robinson, *Economic Heresies*, p. 25.
24. Ibid., p. 33.
25. This is one of Robinson's objections to at least some versions of the marginal productivity doctrine.
26. Joan Robinson, *Accumulation of Capital* (London: Macmillan & Co., 1969), p. 4.
27. Ibid., p. 6.
28. Ibid., pp. 7–8.
29. Ibid., p. 13. Later considerations point up difficulties with the concept of net investment, which leads Robinson to view profit as including amortization for many purposes (ibid., p. 43).
30. Ibid., p. 14.
31. Ibid., p. 311.
32. Ibid., pp. 43–44. Purchases of consumption goods by materials suppliers complete the recovery of costs. Robinson turns the classical surplus notion around in this. There it was the production of a *real* surplus over wages that permitted the appearance of profit. Here it is the existence of an investment sector that allows the *value* of wage-goods to rise beyond the level of wages in that sector, thus producing the possibility of profit (quasi-rent).
33. Ibid., p. 48.

34. Ibid., p. 76.

35. In reference to this kind of consideration, Robinson writes: "The revival of interest in the classical questions brings a revival of the classical theory. Much in the following pages will be startlingly familiar to learned readers. I did not myself arrive at these ideas by studying the classics . . . . But I was very much illuminated by Piero Sraffa's Introduction to Ricardo's *Principles.*" Ibid., p. vi.

36. Ibid., p. 76. Robinson also points out, for later consideration, that stagnation can also arise from consumption of profits as well as financial and monetary problems.

37. Ibid., pp. 241–42.

38. Ibid., p. 192.

39. Robinson, *Economic Heresies*, p. 47.

40. Ibid., p. 48.

41. Robinson, *Accumulation of Capital*, p. 192.

42. Robinson, *Economic Heresies*, p. 48.

43. Ibid., p. 49.

44. Sidney Weintraub, *An Approach to the Theory of Income Distribution* (Philadelphia: Chilton Co., 1958), p. 27.

45. Ibid., p. 48.

46. Ibid., p. 191.

47. Ibid., p. 195.

48. Ibid., p. 198.

49. Ibid., pp. 193–94.

50. Ibid., p. 194.

51. Ibid., p. 202.

52. Ibid., p. 203.

53. Ibid.

54. Ibid., p. 200.

55. Compare Weston, Chapter 6.

56. Weintraub, *An Approach to the Theory of Income Distribution*, p. 200.

57. See Sidney Weintraub, *A General Theory of the Price Level* (Philadelphia: Chilton Co., 1959). Recent trends may invite some modification.

58. Sidney Weintraub, *Keynes and the Monetarists*, p. 141.

59. See esp. Weintraub's "Generalizing Kalecki and Simplifying Macroeconomics," *Journal of Post Keynesian Economics*, Spring 1979, pp. 101–7.

60. Weintraub, *Keynes and the Monetarists*, p. 152.

61. In a more recent, and provocative, formulation, Weintraub finds that "everyone is a 'little right' in share theory." Whether the theory leans to productivity or savings, supply or demand, Weintraub finds justification in focusing on investment, the consumption-wage bill coefficient, output per worker, and monopoly power. See his "An Eclectic Theory of Income Shares," *Journal of Post Keynesian Economics*, Fall 1981, p. 23.

62. Weintraub, *Keynes and the Monetarists*, pp. 167–68.

CHAPTER 11

Profits: A Concluding Assessment

The purpose of studying economics is not to acquire a set of ready-made answers to economic questions, but to learn how to avoid being deceived by economists.

—*Joan Robinson*

The Post Keynesian profit reconstruction as here developed may be summarized in the following four propositions:

1. The first income distinction is between income from labor and income from property, a distinction that arises from the institution of private ownership of productive resources in a capitalist economy. Property income (and a portion of the labor income) can be regarded as the production surplus—that is, as part of the net output over and above costs (including the cost of reproducing the labor force). Profit, therefore, is part of the surplus.

2. The second distinction is between contractual and noncontractual incomes. The former include wage, interest, and rent payments; profits stem from the latter.

3. Production, distribution, and exchange are time-consuming processes occurring in an uncertain world. Producers can adjust to the activities of other producers and consumers, but they cannot do so instantaneously. Furthermore, the decision to invest in capital equipment is nonreversible. Imputed values of contractual productive factors can be computed, if at all, only *after* the fact, and hence

are not useful for determining incomes. A profit residual will therefore generally appear.

4. For products to be sold at prices that allow profit to exist (indeed, that allow property incomes in general to exist), there must be a demand component other than that derived from wages. In particular, other entrepreneurs must be consuming and/or investing.

These four elements are fused together in a new paradigm, not as an eclectic amalgam, but as a consistent and coherent approach to the uncovering of the profit magnitude. On this basis profits can be viewed as an integral and necessary part of the capitalist economy, not as an aberration or a temporary disequilibrium phenomenon, and can be seen to arise from real processes rather than imagined ones.

This analysis of profit origin does not automatically resolve all issues, but it does develop a framework with which to approach further investigation. Still to be clarified, for example, is the relation between the residual income and imputed factor payments. For proprietorships, in which all incomes are jumbled together, there might be a sensible distinction to be made; in a corporation, which has both borrowed and owned capital, and where executives' apparent labor incomes are often directly related to the corporation's net income, imputed payments of factors may not be identifiable or meaningful. More generally, Weintraub's perception that the activity that generates profits may be separated from the sharing of profits needs to be further examined. The related issue of locating entrepreneurial activity in a corporation is likewise in need of clarification. Last, the tricky issue of the profit *rate* must be tackled. Profits are residual incomes not attributable to any well-defined, transferable productive "factor," hence the rate of profit cannot be given the same kind of meaning as the wage rate, the interest rate, or rent (expressed as a rate—for example, rent per acre). It is nevertheless possible that a significant though discrepant meaning can be attached to this expression. This profit reconstruction has promise not only for profit theory but also for economic theory in general.

The same cannot be said of all recent attempts to account for profit. There are lessons to be learned in the history of profit theory, but they are too often ignored, as the following representative examples indicate.

BRONFENBRENNER'S "NAIVE" THEORY

Martin Bronfenbrenner proposes to resurrect "naive profit theory," which he judges to be a compromise between Frank Knight's theoretical position and the practical view that equates profit to business net income.

The "naive" theory, according to Bronfenbrenner, has generally been identified by five propositions.

(1) One of the distributive shares in a competitive economy is normal profits. (2) These are usually positive in the long run, even net of implicit returns to inputs supplied by entrepreneurs to their own firms. (3) Profits are the return to the related entrepreneurial functions of ultimate decision-making and uncertainty-bearing. A maker of ultimate decisions (bearer of ultimate uncertainties) is an "entrepreneur"; entrepreneurs receive all profits in the long run. (4) The quantity that a firm seeks to maximize in its economic operations is the absolute size of the profit component. (5) In marginalist terms, uncertainty-bearing may be regarded as a separate input or factor of production on the same footing as land, labor, or capital.[1]

The naive theory "survives largely as underpinning for policy pronouncements of a capitalist-apologist variety—a fate possibly worse than death."[2] Its eclipse is not complete, however.

It is difficult to profess full satisfaction with Schumpeter, Knight, or the institutional writers. Payments, generally regarded as profits rather than rents, persist without apparent Schumpeterian innovation. Businessmen and promoters persist in estimating profits *ex ante* despite Knightian usage, and the public continues to think of profits as the special income of a special class. At the same time, accountants' "net income" combines elements so numerous, and weighted so differently in different firms, as to cast doubt on the analytical value of institutional theories.[3]

This objection to Knight's uncertainty theory is not well founded; what matters for Knight is not that entrepreneurs expect to make

profits but only that uncertainty as to the outcome prevents entrepreneurs and resource-owners from knowing in advance not only
how large profits will be, but even whether profits or losses will
occur. Furthermore, if popular usage is to be a guide, surely the
classical surplus notion is superior.

In any case, Bronfenbrenner's reformulation accepts Propositions 1 and 2 while dispensing with Proposition 5. Proposition 3 is
greatly modified.

Gone are decision-making and organizing as bases for profit. Limited is
uncertainty-bearing, in its relation to profit, to the assumption of noncontractual positions in the supply of services. As to entrepreneurship, it is
scattered among suppliers of various productive services on entrepreneurial terms. [4]

Further, "Proposition 4 . . . seems to require modification less
from sophisticated theories of profit than from the notions of
'optimizing' rather than 'maximizing' profit." [5]

The key point is that concerning the third proposition. Bronfenbrenner considers entrepreneurial services simply as those which
are rewarded as residual income claimants rather than by contract;
there is nothing functional to distinguish them. Bronfenbrenner
suggests that profit (or loss) can appear only if there is imperfect
competition in the market for these services. Even so, it is hard to
understand how profit can continue to appear except in the
Knightian uncertainty framework; anything else would imply
irrationality on the part of the contractual payment receivers (or on
the part of residual income receivers, in the case of losses)—even
more so if Bronfenbrenner accepts, as he claims, the first proposition which asserts that profits appear regularly in a *competitive*
economy. Instead of limiting Knight, then, Bronfenbrenner gener-
alizes him, making everyone potentially an uncertainty-bearer able
to earn profits. Whatever merit, if any, there might be in this
updating of Wicksell, there is nothing new for profit origin.

LAMBERTON AND THE FIRM

Donald M. Lamberton asserts that the main problem with
profit theory is the "overabstraction which has led to neglect of the

firm, its nature, policy criteria and even its activities."[6] That is, the goals of the firm have not been clearly studied, but rather "incorporated in theory by means of conventional assumptions," or even ignored entirely in favor of the study of the elusive entrepreneur.

He argues for a different view of the firm, one which "goes beyond the substitution of firm for entrepreneur and calls for consideration of the resources which constitute the firm as opposed to those which are purchased by the firm; in particular emphasis is placed upon organization and information."[7] From this it follows that the economic, technological, and organizational sides of the firm are not distinct. Furthermore, the possibility of conventional pricing procedures (such as markup pricing) leads to the importance of alternative profit criteria—alternative, that is, to short-run maximization. Last, uncertainty is not entirely exogenous; the firm may act to reduce uncertainty (not, however, in the probabilistic—or risk—sense). Indeed, non-price competition and monopoly can be viewed as an example of this.[8]

Lamberton also argues that "the subtraction process which reduced profit gradually from the income of the enterprise to the difference between expected and realized income has been carried too far." This, in fact, is the corollary to his view regarding the firm, for "the observed role of the modern large company can be understood only by abandoning the attempt to break such organizations down into their component parts."[9] However, while Lamberton argues cogently for a new analysis of the firm, and much is made of existing empirical studies and suggestions for future ones, no clear analysis emerges regarding profit.[10]

PROFITS AND MONITORS

In a different vein, Armen Alchian and Harold Demsetz provide a theory of the firm, which has implications for profit theory. They assert that an economic organization has two "key demands," namely, the metering of input productivity and the metering of rewards; the task is to ensure such a positive correlation between the two that reduces "shirking" of "team production,"

production in which (1) several types of resources are used and (2) the product is not a sum of separable outputs of each cooperating resource. An additional factor creates a team organization problem—(3) not all resources used in team production belong to one person. [11]

They conjecture that the situation is not the one which economic theory commonly assumes—and analyzes—namely, that "productivity automatically creates its own reward," but rather the reverse: "the specific system of rewarding which is relied upon stimulates a particular productivity response." [12] This conjecture, based on the inability to observe marginal products in team production, runs counter to marginal productivity theory, a thought that is not pursued. In arguing that the "costs of metering or ascertaining the marginal products of the team's members is what calls forth new organization and procedures," however, they add another dimension to the issue: information is available, but not freely. [13]

Their essential conclusion is that the most economical solution to this metering problem produces the "classical firm." One of the "team members" is assigned the special function of "monitoring" the performance (i.e., the shirking) of the other members. The problem of "monitoring the monitor" is solved by assigning to him the profit residual. He earns this residual through the reduction in shirking he brings about. [14] Therefore the classical firm

is identified here as a contractual structure with: (1) joint input production; (2) several input owners; (3) one party who is common to all contracts of the joint inputs; (4) who has rights to renegotiate any input's contract independently of contracts with other input owners; (5) who holds the residual claim; and (6) who has the right to sell his central contractual residual status. The central agent is called the firm's owner and the employer. [15]

Regardless of whether the firm genuinely emerged as a response to some propensity for shirking work, this emphasis on contracts and the profit residual is at least suggestive for profit theory. Unfortunately, here too the existence of profits is *assumed*, not explained. This would appear to be, at least in part, the result of the focus on activity *within* the firm, rather than in its interaction with other firms and consumers. This focus opens the way for the marginal productivity criticism: if the firm provides incentives which elicit certain productivity responses, there is no particular reason for marginal products and factor payments to differ. A profit residual would then emerge only if factor-owners were unaware of their own marginal products. This case of incomplete information to the factor-owners but (more) complete information to the residual income claimant would seem to be a true exploitation situation. [16]

There is an important issue here. Alchian, in an earlier work, seemed to distill profits from imperfect foresight. Thus,

positive profits . . . are the mark of success and viability. It does not matter through what process of reasoning or motivation such success was achieved. . . . Also, the greater the uncertainties of the world, the greater is the possibility that profits would go to venturesome and lucky rather than to logical, careful, fact-gathering individuals. [17]

But uncertainty in the Knightian sense implies that there are many things about the future that *cannot* be known, which conflicts with the view of Alchian and Demsetz in arguing that the monitor's income, the profit residual, arises from unknown, but knowable, quantities. But in this case, that the monitor receives positive income is proof that one of the other income recipients is being paid *less* than his productive contribution; it is, therefore, a tip-off that an investment in acquiring this type of information would also yield a positive return. In that case, the profit income would be eliminated.

WOOD'S FINANCIAL PROFITS

Adrian Wood seeks to explain not so much why profits appear but rather how large they are. Weston remarks that instead of the book's actual title—*A Theory of Profits*—"a more informative title of the book would be 'Some Extensions of Corporate Financial Models Under the Sales Maximization Hypothesis.' "[18] This does indicate Wood's emphasis. Like Lamberton, he focuses attention first on the firm—in this case, the corporation—with the aim being to determine the share of profits in national income and executed through aggregation over all corporations.

Profits for Wood are gross of interest, depreciation, and taxation, but net of nontrading income (i.e., returns on the firm's financial assets). More important, profits are the main source of finance for investment. In fact, "the amount of profits which a company plans to earn is determined by the amount of investment that it intends to undertake."[19] This conclusion buttresses a non-neoclassical, even anti-neoclassical, view of financial markets and their relation to the firm. Wood's notion of the firm is equally so, not only in his assertion that sales maximization is the firm's goal, but also with respect to the difference between long-run and short-run (and their relation), and to some extent the financial aspects of corporate policy. He argues,

Industrial and commercial companies set their prices on the basis of a proportional mark-up on unit costs, the latter being calculated at normal full capacity use, and . . . the size of the mark-up is invariant with respect to short run changes in the degree of capacity use.[20]

The determinants of the markup must then be found. Specifically, Wood argues that the firm tries to maximize its sales subject to the constraints of the "opportunity frontier" and the "financial frontier." The former relates to the investment opportunities of a firm, the latter to the availability of finance of a firm.

This approach is not equally well designed to explain the *source* of profits (in an economic sense rather than an accounting one). The opportunity frontier cannot be made into a macroeconomic concept, hence recourse must be made to equilibrium growth to help make the model determinate (though Wood also discusses disequilibrium). Unfortunately, however, the model loses some of its explanatory prowess in the implementation.[21] And in any case, what results is how large profits *must be*, in the model, rather than the reason for any profits at all. On the key issue of profit origin, Wood has little to offer.

PROFITS AND GENERAL EQUILIBRIUM

In mainstream economic theory, general equilibrium (GE) models still rule the roost. Much has been done since Walras, especially in the realm of refinement, but some substantive material has also appeared. Nevertheless, the evolution remains dubious for profit theory, as GEs cling to the "no-profit" equilibrium condition as the normal state of the economy. Whatever their merits, these constructs cannot be said to be a useful realistic picture of the operation of a capitalist economy.

The implications of this conclusion are far-reaching, as a growing number of critics suggest. Martin Shubik, for example, argues,

the general equilibrium analysis is excellent for studying certain aspects of the efficient allocation of resources in an economy in equilibrium run by a price system. But it provides a conceptual straightjacket which makes it poorly suited for dealing with complex information conditions or with states of disequilibrium.[22]

The three major flaws he sees are: (1) the independence of these models from the number of competitors; (2) the unrealism of the information requirements (i.e., there is too much information freely available); and (3) the static character of general equilibrium. It is necessary to incorporate into the theory money, time, and information/uncertainty.[23]

John R. Hicks also argues for the inclusion of time, "real time," in economic theory.[24] Without thinking "*in* time," analysis remains in the rut of static and stationary states. Furthermore, it is necessary to "assume that people in one's models do not know what is going to happen, and know that they do not know what is going to happen."[25] This sort of uncertainty breaks down the mechanistic, timeless determinism of general equilibrium.

The model presented by Kenneth Arrow and Frank H. Hahn points out a more serious difficulty. Although both money and the money wage (a contract) enter into this framework—albeit in the last chapter, "The Keynesian Model"—it is nonetheless true, as they indicate, that their economy is "still only a distant relative of the economy we know. . . . In particular, the absence of production in our analysis so far is significant."[26] Elsewhere they argue that in a "pure-exchange economy" relatively "modest" assumptions permit convergence to equilibrium, and they declare that "if we wish to maintain that in many situations the process of decentralized decisions is not convergent, it is likely that we shall have to look for the causes on the 'production side.' This in itself is valuable information."[27] It may be valuable, but it is hardly surprising. In any case, Hahn finds justification for general equilibrium theory mainly in a negative sense: the theory carefully identifies the assumptions required to draw the usual neoclassical conclusions and policy recommendations, but he makes it clear that these assumptions do not hold in the real-world economy.[28]

Nonetheless, Hahn appears to agree with E. Roy Weintraub's assessment that general equilibrium theory is in a healthy state.

the theory has been responsive to changes in the way economists have viewed current problems, and this responsiveness has facilitated the use of general equilibrium analysis in many areas of applied economics. This two-way interaction is probably the best indicator that the concerns of Smith, Cournot, Walras, Pareto, and Edgeworth are still alive, and lively today.[29]

These concerns include the attempt to provide models of private-ownership economic systems in which "the interdependence of producing and consuming agents is identified," that is, production is to be included.[30] Profits have still not made their appearance, however. "If answers are emerging only slowly, it is because the problems are difficult and not because general equilibrium theorists have failed to ask hard questions."[31]

The profit problem is indeed difficult, but need not be as vexing and formidable as general equilibrium models would make it. It was precisely the point of classical economic theory to emphasize the fundamental role of production in beginning the circular flow of economic activity which was embodied in the surplus notion. And the Walrasian scheme of marginal productivity incomes has already shown its vacuousness regarding profit origin. The time-consuming character of economic activity in a changing, uncertain world is dissipated. It is unreasonable, and a hopeless flaw, to look for a profit process within the equilibrium straightjacket.

PROFIT THEORY AND CAPITALISM

The post-Keynesian profit analysis may not be the only possible consistent and coherent account of the appearance of profits in a capitalist economy; work along other lines may yet prove fruitful. But of the existing approaches, it alone seems to have drawn the appropriate conclusions from the history of attempts at profit explanation. Indispensable in formulatng meaningful theory, these conclusions may be profitably summarized.

In the first place, the view of the economy as a system in equilibrium, where expectations are met, and where everyone therefore knows in advance the results of production and exchange, leaves no room for profits. Any potential residual income is quickly squandered, in these schemes, by an increase in production in the relevant area, resulting in lower output prices and higher costs, thus squeezing out profits. Productive resources may be scarce, but entrepreneurs are not, hence they do not receive income for any special productive contribution. Of course, with the future known by all, these entrepreneurs also make no special contribution. Ostensibly, this way of depicting the economy merely evades most, if not all, interesting, important, and intricate questions.

Marginal productivity theory has been criticized as inadequate as a theory of income distribution in general, and most particularly as a theory of profit. Here income is paid according to the productive contribution of the last unit of each productive factor. Yet in the case of capital (and possibly also in the case of land and labor) it is impossible to aggregate the heterogeneous goods to comprise the productive factor "capital" without already *knowing* the rate at which capital is remunerated: the theory reasons in a circle. Simultaneous determination within the confines of an equilibrium system might offer a way out of the vicious circle in logic, but it also disqualifies marginal productivity as any kind of explanation, degenerating into an "everything determines everything" banality, an especially unenlightening approach to interpreting economic processes. In addition, it raises all the problems for profit theory already indicated.

Even without these problems, marginal productivity is a futile guide to profit theory. The view of profits as a return to a productive factor has more to do with finding a rationale—an apologetic, really—for the profit income than with explaining the operation of the economy. All attempts to identify a productive factor for which profits are paid must founder because of the nature of the problem. If profits are conceived of as the return to capital, the distinction between interest and profit is lost, so that the net income earned by a firm is identical in substance to the cost to that firm of borrowing money. And as the latter clearly excludes any residual income, so must the former, so that neither profit, not any other defined income class, takes account of any residual. Thus residual income vanishes, and creates another logical flaw for this mode of reasoning. The extreme variability of the firm's net income, well recognized as a fact of life in the business world, is associated with a much more stable capital "factor"—which contradicts the assertion of capital as a profit-earning substance. The greater stability of the return to (or income from) borrowed capital, as compared to the firm's return, would also appear to create two rates of return for the same factor. Thus, this approach holds no promise for a theory of profit.

No other profit agent can be found, however. If, for example, the entrepreneur is to receive income for engaging in some activity, such as managing or organizing production, then it is a labor service that is being rewarded, and profits are really a special form of wage. If, on the other hand, the entrepreneur undertakes no such identifiable activity, there is no reason for a profit income to be produced. Furthermore, any profit factor approach must somehow be shown to be responsible for the ever-changing pattern of the firm's (or entrepreneur's) net income. No agent (except in the purely tautological sense) has ever been found which can be correlated with this income pattern.

It has been argued for several centuries that profit is a necessary incentive for the entrepreneur to bother to undertake production. Very likely this is the case, but it is no answer to the question of profit origin, for even those entrepreneurs who end up with losses were lured into their mistakes by the dream of profit. This is precisely the problem to be solved: how is the hope of profit turned into an actual realization of profit?

Equally unhelpful is the suggestion, likewise repeated through the years, that profit is the entrepreneur's reward for the function of bearing risk. Insofar as risk is taken in the probabilistic sense, the gain to one is a loss to another, with profit going not to the function of risk-bearing but simply to good fortune. Furthermore, the widespread use of insurance policies transfers risk away from the firm/entrepreneur, eliminating it as a possibility for anyone but the insurance company. Nonprobabilistic risk, or true uncertainty, is of great consequence, but it is misleading to suggest that the service of bearing uncertainty is what is rewarded with profit. At the very least, uncertainty is immeasurable, and therefore the size of the profit reward is indeterminate. Besides, again, not all those who face uncertainty are rewarded positively; thus uncertainty-bearing would have to be viewed as the source of both profits and losses.

It is precisely this sort of blind alley that profit theory must escape. The means to do so emerge from this very analysis. Economic activity occurs in real time, in an environment whose future course is not and cannot ever be entirely known, since it depends in large part on the decisions of the individuals involved. These decisions, in turn, are vexatious enough for the individuals themselves to make; they are certainly not predictable by others. Contracts, which determine incomes for labor and most owners of land and capital, are set before output is produced, much less sold. The case of rent, interest, and wages exactly exhausting the value of output, leaving no residual income—that is, "no profit"—is clearly a fictitious, illusory occurrence.

Profits emerge as a regular, commonplace, and essential part of the capitalist economy, not as an occasional aberration or disequilibrium phenomenon; to adopt the latter position would kill off equilibrium theory. Profits arise from real processes rather than imaginary or hypothetical processes. Illumination on profit theory has promise not only for profit theory itself but also for the development and refurbishment of all of economic theory.

Notes

1. Martin Bronfenbrenner, *Income Distribution Theory* (Chicago: Aldine Atherton, 1971), pp. 366–67.

2. Ibid., p. 366.

3. Ibid., p. 370.

4. Ibid., p. 380.

5. Ibid.

6. Donald M. Lamberton, *The Theory of Profit* (New York: Augustus M. Kelley, 1969), p. 1.

7. Ibid., p. 41.

8. Ibid., pp. 43, 53.

9. Ibid., p. 198.

10. Sidney Weintraub is only too correct in labeling this work a theory of the firm rather than a theory of profits; see *American Economic Review*, December 1966, p. 1261.

11. Armen A. Alchian and Harold Demsetz, "Production, Information Costs, and Economic Organization," *American Economic Review*, December 1972, p. 779.

12. Ibid., pp. 778–79.

13. Ibid., p. 780. This is also the point of Alchian's "Information Costs, Pricing, and Resource Unemployment," *Economic Inquiry*, June 1969.

14. Alchian and Demsetz, "Production, Information Costs, and Economic Organization," p. 782.

15. Ibid., p. 794.

16. Of course, the employer should be receiving compensation for this work in discovering marginal products, but this would be an income from labor and has nothing to do with profit.

17. Armen A. Alchian, "Uncertainty, Evolution, and Economic Theory," *Journal of Political Economy*, June 1950, p. 213.

18. *Journal of Economic Literature*, December 1976, p. 1280.

19. Adrian Wood, *A Theory of Profits* (Cambridge: Cambridge University Press, 1975), p. 17.

20. Ibid., p. 61.

21. Though the point could be argued that his opportunity frontier concept is too abstract to explain much anyway.

22. Martin Shubik, "The General Equilibrium Model Is Incomplete and Not Adequate for the Reconciliation of Micro and Macro Theory," *Kyklos* 28 (1975): 545.

23. Ibid., pp. 546, 559. See also Martin Shubik, "A Curmudgeon's Guide to Microeconomics," *Journal of Economic Literature*, June 1970, pp. 413–15.

24. John R. Hicks, "Some Questions of Time in Economics," in *Evolution, Welfare, and Time in Economics*, ed. Anthony M. Tang et al. (Lexington, Mass.: D. C. Heath & Co., 1976).

25. John R. Hicks, *Economic Perspectives* (Oxford: Oxford University Press, 1977), p. vii.

26. Kenneth J. Arrow and Frank H. Hahn, *General Competitive Analysis* (San Francisco: Holden-Day, 1971), p. 346.

27. Ibid., p. 325.

28. Frank H. Hahn, *On the Notion of Equilibrium in Economics* (Cambridge: Cambridge University Press, 1973), pp. 14–15.

29. E. Roy Weintraub, "General Equilibrium Theory," in *Modern Economic Thought*, ed. Sidney Weintraub (Philadelphia: University of Pennsylvania Press, 1977), p. 122.

30. Ibid., p. 107.

31. E. Roy Weintraub, "The Microfoundations of Macroeconomics: A Critical Survey," *Journal of Economic Literature*, March 1977, p. 19.

References

Alchian, Armen A. "Information Costs, Pricing, and Resource Unemployment." *Economic Inquiry,* June 1969.
———."Uncertainty, Evolution, and Economic Theory." *Journal of Political Economy,* June 1950.
Alchian, Armen A., and Demsetz, Harold. "Production, Information Costs, and Economic Organization." *American Economic Review,* December 1972.
Arrow, Kenneth J., and Hahn, Frank H. *General Competitive Analysis.* San Francisco: Holden-Day, 1971.
Bailey, Samuel. *A Critical Dissertation on the Nature, Measure, and Causes of Value.* London: R. Hunter, 1825.
Bernstein, Peter. "Profit Theory—Where Do We Go from Here?" *Quarterly Journal of Economics,* August 1953.
Böhm-Bawerk, Eugen von. *Capital and Interest.* South Holland, Ill.: Libertarian Press, 1959.
———. *Karl Marx and the Close of His System.* New York: Macmillan Co., 1898.
Boulding, Kenneth. *A Reconstruction of Economics.* New York: John Wiley & Sons, 1950.
Bronfenbrenner, Martin. *Income Distribution Theory.* Chicago: Aldine Atherton, 1971.
Cantillon, Richard. *Essay on the Nature of Trade in General.* New York: Augustus M. Kelley, 1964.
Chamberlin, Edward. *The Theory of Monopolistic Competition.* Cambridge: Harvard University Press, 1958.
Clark, John Bates. *The Distribution of Wealth.* New York: Macmillan Co., 1899.
———. *Essentials of Economic Theory.* New York: Macmillan Co., 1907.

Commons, John R. *Institutional Economics.* New York: Macmillan Co., 1934.

———. *The Legal Foundations of Capitalism.* New York: Macmillan Co., 1924.

Cournot, Antoine Augustin. *Researches into the Mathematical Principles of the Theory of Wealth.* New York: Augustus M. Kelley, 1960.

Davidson, Paul. *Theories of Aggregate Income Distribution.* New Brunswick, N.J.: Rutgers University Press, 1960.

Dobb, Maurice. *Theories of Value and Distribution Since Adam Smith.* Cambridge: Cambridge University Press, 1973.

Edgeworth, Francis Y. *Papers Relating to Political Economy.* London: Macmillan & Co., 1925.

Eichner, Alfred, ed. *A Guide to Post-Keynesian Economics.* White Plains, N.Y.: M. E. Sharpe, 1979.

Erdos, Peter, and Molnar, Ferenc. "Profit and Paper Profit: Some Kalecki Evolution." *Journal of Post Keynesian Economics,* Fall 1980.

Feiwel, George. *The Intellectual Capital of Michal Kalecki.* Knoxville: University of Tennessee Press, 1975.

Fellner, William. *Probability and Profit.* Homewood, Ill.: Richard Irwin, 1965.

Fellner, William, and Haley, Bernard F., eds. *Readings in the Theory of Income Distribution.* Philadelphia: Blakiston Co., 1946.

Galbraith, John Kenneth. *The New Industrial State.* Boston: Houghton Mifflin Co., 1967.

Hahn, Frank H. *On the Notion of Equilibrium in Economics.* Cambridge: Cambridge University Press, 1973.

Harcourt, Geoffrey C. *Some Cambridge Controversies in the Theory of Capital.* Cambridge: Cambridge University Press, 1972.

Hawley, Frederick B. *Enterprise and the Productive Process.* New York: Knickerbocker Press, 1907.

———. "The Fundamental Error of 'Kapital und Kapitalzins.'" *Quarterly Journal of Economics,* April 1892.

———. "Profits and the Residual Theory." *Quarterly Journal of Economics,* July 1890.

———. "Reply to Final Objections to the Risk Theory of Profit." *Quarterly Journal of Economics,* August 1901.

Hicks, J. R. *Economic Perspectives.* Oxford: Oxford University Press, 1977.

Hobson, John A. *The Industrial System.* London: Longman, Green & Co., 1910.

Hollander, Samuel. *The Economics of David Ricardo.* Toronto: University of Toronto Press, 1979.

Hume, David. *Writings on Economics.* Edited by Eugene Rotwein. Edinburgh: Thomas Nelson & Sons, 1955.

Hunt, E. K. *History of Economic Thought: A Critical Perspective.* Belmont, Calif.: Wadsworth Publishing Co., 1979.

Jaffé, William. "Another Look at Leon Walras's Theory of Tâtonnement." *History of Political Economy,* Summer 1981.

Jevons, William Stanley. *The Theory of Political Economy.* Middlesex, Eng.: Penguin Books, 1970.

Kaldor, Nicholas. "The Equilibrium of the Firm." *Economic Journal,* March 1934.

———. *Essays in Value and Distribution.* Glencoe, Ill.: Free Press, 1960.

Kalecki, Michal. *Essays in the Theory of Economic Fluctuations.* New York: Russell & Russell, 1972.

———. *Selected Essays on the Dynamics of the Capitalist Economy, 1933-1970.* Cambridge: Cambridge University Press, 1971.

———.*Studies in the Theory of Business Cycles, 1933-1939.* New York: Augustus M. Kelley, 1966.

Keirstead, B. S. *Capital, Interest, and Profits.* New York: John Wiley & Sons, 1959.

———. *The Theory of Profits and Income Distribution.* Oxford: Basil Blackwell, 1953.

Keynes, John Maynard. *Essays in Persuasion,* vol. 9 of *Collected Writings.* London: Macmillan & Co., 1972.

———. *The General Theory of Employment, Interest, and Money.* New York: Harcourt, Brace & World & Co. 1964.

———. *A Treatise on Money.* London: Macmillan & Co., 1965.

Knight, Frank. *Risk, Uncertainty, and Profit.* Chicago: University of Chicago Press, 1971.

Kregel, Jan. *Rate of Profit, Distribution and Growth: Two Views.* Chicago and New York: Aldine Atherton, 1971.

———. *The Reconstruction of Political Economy.* New York: John Wiley & Sons, 1973.

Lamberton, Donald M. *The Theory of Profit.* New York: Augustus M. Kelley, 1969.

Lange, Oskar. *Political Economy.* Translated by A. H. Walker. London and New York: Pergamon Press, 1974.

Locke, John. *Some Considerations of the Consequences of the Lowering of Interest and Raising the Value of Money.* London: Awnsham & John Churchill, 1969.

Malthus, Thomas Robert. *Definitions in Political Economy.* London: John Murray, 1827.

———. *Principles of Political Economy.* New York: Augustus M. Kelley, 1951.

Marshall, Alfred. *Principles of Economics.* New York: Macmillan Co., 1948.

Marx, Karl. *Capital.* New York: International Publishers, 1967.

———. *A Contribution to the Critique of Political Economy.* New York: International Publishers, 1970.

————. *Theories of Surplus Value*. Moscow: Progress Publishers, 1963.

Massie, Joseph. *An Essay on the Governing Causes of the Natural Rate of Interest*. London: W. Own, 1750.

Meek, Ronald. *Studies in the Labor Theory of Value*. New York: Monthly Review Press, 1956.

Mill, John Stuart. *Principles of Political Economy*. Fairfield, N.J.: Augustus M. Kelley, 1976.

North, Dudley. *Discourses upon Trade*. London: Thomas Bassett, 1691.

Petty, William. *The Economic Writings of Sir William Petty*. Cambridge: Cambridge University Press, 1899.

Pierson, Nikolaas G. *Principles of Economics*. London: Macmillan & Co., 1902.

de Quincey, Thomas. *The Logic of Political Economy*. Edinburgh and London: William Blackwood & Sons, 1844.

Ricardo, David. *The Works and Correspondence of David Ricardo*. Edited by Piero Sraffa. Cambridge: Cambridge University Press, 1951.

Robinson, Joan. *Accumulation of Capital*. London: Macmillan & Co., 1969.

————. *Collected Economic Papers*. Oxford: Basil Blackwell, 1951, 1965, 1973.

————. *Economic Heresies*. New York: Basic Books, 1971.

————. *The Economics of Imperfect Competition*. London: Macmillan & Co., 1959.

Robinson, Joan, and Eatwell, John. *An Introduction to Modern Economics*. London: McGraw-Hill Book Co., 1973.

Roncaglia, Alessandro, "Hollander's Ricardo." *Journal of Post Keynesian Economics*, Spring 1982.

————. "Sraffa and the Reconstruction of Political Economy." *Challenge*, January–February 1979.

————. *Sraffa and the Theory of Prices*. New York: John Wiley & Sons, 1978.

Roscher, Wilhelm. *Principles of Political Economy*. New York: Henry Holt & Co., 1878.

Samuelson, Paul. *Economics*. 9th ed. New York: McGraw-Hill Book Co., 1973.

Say, Jean-Baptiste. *Treatise on Political Economy*. Philadelphia: J. B. Lippincott Co. , 1860.

Schumpeter, Joseph. *The Theory of Economic Development*. Cambridge: Harvard University Press, 1961.

Senior, Nassau. *An Outline of the Science of Political Economy*. New York: Augustus M. Kelley, 1951.

Shackle, G. L. S. *Keynesian Kaleidics*. Edinburgh: Edinburgh University Press, 1974.

Shubik, Martin. "A Curmudgeon's Guide to Microeconomics." *Journal of Economic Literature*, June 1970.

————. "The General Equilibrium Model Is Incomplete and Not Adequate for the Reconciliation of Micro and Macro Theory," *Kyklos* 28 (1975).

Smith, Adam. *Wealth of Nations.* New York: Modern Library, 1965.

Sowell, Thomas. *Say's Law: An Historical Introduction.* Princeton: Princeton University Press, 1972.

Sraffa, Piero. "The Laws of Returns Under Competitive Conditions." *Economic Journal,* December 1926.

————. *Production of Commodities by Means of Commodities.* Cambridge: Cambridge University Press, 1960.

Steuart, James. *An Inquiry into the Principles of Political Economy.* Chicago: University of Chicago Press, 1966.

Stevenson, Harold, and Nelson, J. Russell, eds. *Profits in the Modern Economy.* Minneapolis: University of Minnesota Press, 1967.

Tang, Anthony M., et al., eds. *Evolution, Welfare, and Time in Economics.* Essays in Honor of N. Georgescu-Roegen. Lexington, Mass.: D. C. Heath & Co., 1976.

Thünen, Johann Heinrich von. *Ausgewählte Texte.* Meisenheim, Federal Republic of Germany: Westkulturverlag Anton Haim, 1951.

Triffin, Robert. *Monopolistic Competition and General Equilibrium Theory.* Cambridge: Harvard University Press, 1962.

Turgot, Anne Robert Jacques. *Turgot on Progress, Sociology, and Economics.* Edited by Ronald L. Meek. Cambridge: Cambridge University Press, 1973.

Veblen, Thorstein. *Absentee Ownership and Business Enterprise in Recent Times.* New York: B. W. Huebsch, 1923.

————. *The Place of Science in Modern Civilization and Other Essays.* New York: B. W. Huebsch, 1919.

————. *Theory of Business Enterprise.* New York: Charles Scribner's Sons, 1904.

Walras, Leon. *Elements of Pure Economics.* London: Allen & Unwin, 1954.

Weintraub, E. Roy. "The Microfoundations of Macroeconomics: A Critical Survey." *Journal of Economic Literature,* March 1977.

Weintraub, Sidney. *An Approach to the Theory of Income Distribution.* Philadelphia: Chilton Co., 1958.

————. *A General Theory of the Price Level.* Philadelphia: Chilton Co., 1959.

————. *Keynes and the Monetarists.* New Brunswick, N.J.: Rutgers University Press, 1973.

————. "Generalizing Kalecki and Simplifying Macroeconomics." *Journal of Post Keynesian Economics,* Spring 1979.

————, ed. *Modern Economic Thought.* Philadelphia: University of Pennsylvania Press, 1977.

―――. "An Eclectic Theory of Income Shares." *Journal of Post Keynesian Economics,* Spring 1981.

Weston, J. Fred. "A Generalized Uncertainty Theory of Profit." *American Economic Review,* March 1950.

Wicksell, Knut. *Lectures on Political Economy.* New York: Macmillan Co., 1934–35.

―――. *Selected Papers on Economic Theory.* Edited by Erik Lindahl. Cambridge: Harvard University Press, 1958.

―――. *Value, Capital, and Rent.* London: Allen & Unwin, 1954.

Wicksteed, Philip. *Coordination of the Laws of Distribution.* London: Macmillan & Co., 1894.

Wood, Adrian. *A Theory of Profits.* Cambridge: Cambridge University Press, 1975.

Young, Allyn. "Increasing Returns and Economic Progress." *Economic Journal,* December 1928.

Index

abstinence, 18, 19, 22, 27
Alchian, Armen A., 157–59, 167, 169
Arrow, Kenneth A., 161, 168, 169

Bailey, Samuel, 37, 169
Bernstein, Peter, 9, 169
Böhm-Bawerk, Eugen von, 34, 38, 40, 50, 51, 63, 69, 169
Boulding, Kenneth, 122–27, 132, 169
Bronfenbrenner, Martin, 90, 155–56, 167, 169

Cantillon, Richard, 11, 12, 15, 24, 28, 169
capital reversal, 110–11
Chamberlin, Edward H., 108, 113, 169
Clark, John Bates, 44–48, 51, 60, 169
Commons, John R., 94–97, 98–99, 101, 102, 169
competition, 21, 36, 39, 40, 46, 47, 55, 60, 65, 71, 72, 79–81, 88, 101, 104–9, 134, 147, 149, 157, 161
contracts, 72, 77–79, 87–89, 93–97, 100, 127, 140, 144–45, 148–49, 153, 156, 158, 165
corporations, 7, 20, 44, 54, 66, 81–83, 97, 99–100, 149, 154, 160
Cournot, Augustin A., 50, 106, 162, 170

Davidson, Paul, 151, 170
degree of monopoly, 129, 135–37, 151

Demsetz, Harold, 157–59, 167, 169
derived demand, 40, 50, 53–54
Dobb, Maurice, 24, 37, 50, 170

Edgeworth, F. Y., 51, 162, 170
entrepreneurs, 3, 4, 11, 15, 16, 20, 21, 27, 40–44, 46–49, 52–68, 77–86, 97–101, 114, 116–21, 128, 138–42, 145–46, 149, 154–57, 163–65
equilibrium, 3, 40–44, 52–54, 61–63, 66–67, 69, 71, 72, 93, 97, 103, 105, 107, 109, 115, 120–22, 133, 135, 141, 145, 160–64, 166
exploitation, 21, 32, 36, 159

Feiwel, George, 150, 170
Fellner, William, 90, 150, 170
Fisher, Irving, 51

Galbraith, John K., 102, 170

Hahn, Frank H., 133, 161, 168, 170
Harcourt, Geoffrey C., 9, 170
Hawley, Frederick B., 63–67, 69, 73, 170
Hicks, John R., 90, 120, 161, 168
Hobson, John A., 94, 99–101, 102, 170
Hollander, Samuel, 37, 170
Hume, David, 11, 24, 170
Hunt, E. K., 51

innovation, 5, 45, 60–63, 86, 155

insurance, 3, 20, 54, 55, 58, 59, 64, 74, 87, 165

Jaffé, William, 50, 170
Jevons, William Stanley, 40, 50, 103, 170

Kaldor, Nicholas, 69, 70, 127-30, 132, 137, 151, 171
Kalecki, Michal, 38, 119, 129, 130, 132-38, 141, 146, 149, 150-52, 171
Keirstead, Burton S., 86, 91, 171
Keynes, John Maynard, 18, 71, 115-23, 127-34, 149, 171
Knight, Frank, x, 25, 47, 51, 54, 64, 71-91, 93-94, 98, 146, 155-56, 159, 171
Kregel, Jan, 114, 171

Lamberton, Donald M., 156-57, 159, 167, 171
Lange, Oskar, 150, 171
Locke, John, 11, 24, 171

Malthus, Thomas R., 17-18, 25, 131, 171
management, 14, 20, 53-58, 64, 75, 80, 100, 122
marginal productivity, 45-46, 52, 53, 66-67, 71, 93, 103, 108, 111, 112, 130, 133, 148-49, 158-59, 163-64
Marshall, Alfred, 14, 25, 50, 51, 53-56, 59, 68, 85, 103, 104, 107, 108, 113, 116-17, 120, 134, 143, 171
Marx, Karl, 2, 13, 18, 24-28, 32-38, 61, 69, 110-11, 114, 115, 129, 138, 171
Massie, Joseph, 24, 171
Meek, Ronald L., 24, 38, 172
Menger, Carl, 40
Mill, John Stuart, 14, 21-23, 25, 26, 85, 106, 172
monopoly, 2, 4, 14, 47, 60, 62, 66, 67, 86, 88, 99, 105-9, 116, 135, 147-49, 157

Niebyl, Karl, xi
North, Dudley, 10, 24, 172

Petty, William, 10, 24, 172

Pierson, Nikolaas, 57-60, 68, 172

quasi-rent, 53, 88, 100, 119, 140-42, 151
Quesnay, François, 24
de Quincey, Thomas, 37, 172

reswitching, 111
Ricardo, David, 21, 25-33, 37, 85, 103, 106, 110-12, 119, 129, 131, 172
risk, 2, 11, 22, 40, 43, 54, 55, 57-59, 62-67, 72-75, 87, 121, 129, 145, 165
Robinson, Joan, x, 25, 50, 51, 69, 90, 107, 113, 131, 138-43, 146, 149-53, 172
Roncaglia, Alessandro, 37, 113, 114, 172
Roscher, Wilhelm, 56-58, 68, 172

Samuelson, Paul, 9, 38, 172
Say, J. B., 13, 15-17, 25, 172
Schumpeter, Joseph, 60-63, 66, 67, 69, 70, 109, 155, 172
Senior, Nassau, 18-19, 21-23, 25, 27, 172
Shackle, G. L. S., 86, 131, 172
Shubik, Martin, 161, 168, 172
Smith, Adam, x, 1, 9, 10, 12-15, 17, 21, 24, 25, 27, 106, 113, 162, 173
Sowell, Thomas, 25, 173
Sraffa, Piero, 37, 103-14, 134, 135, 150, 152, 173
Steuart, James, 12, 24, 173
surplus, 13, 14, 21, 22, 27-36, 39, 56-57, 60, 62, 78, 84, 109-12, 133, 139, 141-42, 145, 151, 153
surplus value, 3, 32-35, 38, 103, 138

Thünen, Johann Heinrich von, 20-21, 25, 27, 51, 57, 173
time, 43, 44, 46, 76, 79, 122, 153, 161
Triffin, Robert, 108, 114, 173
Turgot, A. R. J., 11, 24, 173

uncertainty, 3, 7, 11, 35-36, 43-44, 47, 58, 64, 67, 71-90, 108, 119-20, 122, 133, 142-46, 149, 153, 155-57, 159, 161-62, 165

Veblen, Thorstein, 39, 94-99, 101, 102, 173

waiting, 25, 53
Walras, Leon, 40–44, 50, 51, 53, 67,
  85, 103, 120, 134, 160–62, 173
Weintraub, E. Roy, 162, 168, 173
Weintraub, Sidney, x, xi, 50, 132,
  143–49, 150, 152, 154, 167, 168, 173
Weston, J. Fred, 9, 87–89, 91, 160, 173

Wicksell, Knut, 47–51, 156, 174
Wicksteed, Philip, 51, 174
widow's cruse, 116, 118–19, 121, 123,
  129
Wood, Adrian, 9, 159–60, 167, 174

Young, Allyn, 113, 174

Post Keynesian Economics

Sidney Weintraub and Marvin Goodstein, eds., *Reaganomics in the Stagflation Economy*
Mark Obrinsky. *Profit Theory and Capitalism*